CATHOLICS AND THE NEW AGE

Catholics and the New Age

*How Good People Are Being Drawn into
Jungian Psychology, the Enneagram,
and the Age of Aquarius*

Mitch Pacwa, S.J.

CHARIS

Servant Publications
Ann Arbor, Michigan

Scripture passages in this work have been translated from
the original biblical languages by the author.

Published by Servant Publications
P.O. Box 8617
Ann Arbor, Michigan 48107

Published with the permission of Superiors
Reverend Bradley M. Schaefer, S.J.
Provincial, Chicago Province of the Society of Jesus, 1991.

Cover design by Michael Andaloro

95 10 9 8 7 6

Printed in the United States of America
ISBN 0-89283-756-X

Library of Congress Cataloging-in-Publication Data

Pacwa, Mitch.
    Catholics and the New Age : how good people are being drawn
into Jungian psychology, the enneagram, and the Age of Aquarius /
Mitch Pacwa.
        p.   cm.
Includes bibliographical references.
ISBN 0-89283-756-X
1. Occultism—Religious aspects—Catholic Church.   2. New Age
movement—Controversial literature.   3. Catholic Church—
Doctrines.   4. Enneagram.   I. Title.
BX1789.5P.33   1992
261.5'1—dc20   91-42792

To my father, Mitchell C. Pacwa, Sr.,
on his seventieth birthday, December 26, 1991.

Dad, an intelligent man with an eighth-grade education, encouraged me to study hard at school so that I would not have to work as hard as he did. More importantly, he wanted me to realize how little anyone knows and how much more everyone can learn in this life. This is in appreciation for his hard work that made it possible for me to attend school and for giving me a desire always to learn more.

Contents

NOTE TO THE READER

The reader may find it helpful to keep the following three issues in mind, while reading *Catholics and the New Age*:

First, the author, who is a Scripture scholar, has freshly translated the Scripture passages in this work from the original biblical languages. He has not used an existing version of Scripture.

Second, especially in the first six chapters of the book, the author draws heavily upon his own personal knowledge and experience in describing certain elements of the New Age Movement. In particular, he focuses on Hinduism, Jungian psychology, astrology, and the enneagram. Some readers may wish to use this earlier material selectively, focusing more on what is of particular concern to them in their own situations.

Third, of necessity, the author introduces many technical and theological terms throughout the text. To aid in understanding, the author has provided a glossary of terms. The reader may find frequent use of this glossary helpful as he or she reads *Catholics and the New Age*.

Introduction

A CAMPUS CHAPLAIN at a Catholic university recommends crystals, the energy source of Atlantis, for personal help.

A Catholic women's college offers workshops in Wicca (witchcraft) and the goddess within. Astrology columns appear in the school paper.

"Thoroughly Modern Medium," the title of a lead article which appeared in the 1990 Halloween edition of the Chicago Tribune's Tempo section, describes a spiritist as she addresses the widows' support group about spiritism at St. Peter's parish library. A photo shows elderly Catholics with eyes closed, waiting for spirit contacts with deceased loved ones and friends.

A Chicago parish hosts a professional astrologer to lecture on the stars and inform parishioners where they can go for further astrological consultations.

A catechist objects to her required textbook because it uses the term "mantras" for Catholic aspirations. The pastor demands that she call these prayers mantras or else be fired. She is fired.

A Franciscan convent offers "enlightenment" classes that include Wicca (witchcraft), *I Ching* (Chinese fortune-telling), and Oriental meditation. The sisters staff "The Christine Center for Meditation," teaching yoga, astrology, and Tarot card readings.

Several Carmelite religious offer retreats combining

Carmelite spirituality with Theravadan Buddhist traditions of vipassana (insight) meditation, which are "compatible with any religious affiliation" and "require no belief commitments."

Fr. Justin Belitz, O.F.M., advertises retreats on the *Tao Te Ching* to teach "passive meditation," the "most valuable and important kind of mental prayer." The retreat promises to help one come "in contact with the Divine Presence in you, so that infinite peace, deep joy, all knowledge and wisdom, can flood your life and give it true meaning."

Catholic retreat houses and parishes nationwide offer enneagram workshops conducted by priests and nuns.

What are Catholics to make of all these New Age practices at parishes, retreat houses, universities, and colleges? Why are they attracting so many Catholics today, especially clergy and religious? Are these practices legitimate expressions of spirituality for Catholics? Or do they run counter to the Catholic faith?

This book approaches these questions and issues autobiographically because I, like so many contemporaries in the 1960s and 1970s, dabbled in occult practices now called New Age. Studying the psychology of Dr. Carl G. Jung brought me into an involvement with practices like the *I Ching* and astrology. Jung used the occult in a scientific way. Why could I not use it too? Before long I found myself dabbling in astrology, the enneagram, and Eastern meditation. And I was a Jesuit seminarian studying for the priesthood!

But before I describe my own journey into and out of the New Age, we need a working definition and a short history of the movement.

WHAT IS THE NEW AGE MOVEMENT?

I propose a concise and dense definition here, with an explanation of each point in the following paragraphs. NAM (shorthand for "New Age Movement") is a loosely structured, eclectic movement based on experiences of monism that lead people to believe in pantheism, with a tendency to hold millennarian views of history. We can take this definition apart to see exactly what it means.

First, NAM is loosely structured, with no evidence of a highly organized affiliation or association. Some authors, notably pioneers of Christian research into NAM (Constance Cumbey, Texe Marrs, and Dave Hunt) apparently believe that NAM is a conspiracy to take over the world. Certainly some New Age authors describe an "Aquarian Conspiracy" and a mass awakening of consciousness in the world. They would like to believe they are the unstoppable trend of the future.

Much evidence points to NAM's growing influence in Western society. The media supports and promulgates New Age ideology through movies like *ET, Star Wars,* and *Defend Your Life,* television shows like *Star Trek: the Next Generation,* and even New Age radio stations. Still the data do not show that New Agers are organized enough to agree among themselves about the goals, strategies, or ideals of the whole movement. Sometimes smaller organizations help each other with networks of information and common interest, but these liaisons break down quickly after their common goal is accomplished. Other instances show that jealous greed and competition for customers turns otherwise mellow folk into fierce competitors. One New Age teacher, after having made a million dollars through marketing meditation techniques, was sued by other New Agers and ended up owing half a million dollars. When listening to her own meditation tapes did not change this "downer" reality, she searched for answers. This search brought her home to Christ and the Catholic church.

The New Age Movement is not a cult per se. Some New Age cults exist, but the loose organization of the movement prevents it from being a true cult. Cults depend on leaders who claim absolute (sometimes divine) authority over the lives of their followers. Their messages derive from direct contact with gods and spirits or from their own divine nature. People outside the cult system cannot be saved until they join the ingroup. Affiliation with the cult personality is more important than his or her ideas since the ideas change as the spirits lead them. This description does not fit most New Agers.

Instead of attachment to authority figures, New Agers usually desire ideas and practices to help them cope better with life. They are often too individualistic for cults, desiring the realization of their own personal divinity more than paying obeisance to some leader's divinity. Therefore, they tend to shy away from cultic organizations, though some New Age cults exist.

Second, NAM is highly eclectic; borrowing ideas and practices from many sources. Meditation techniques from Hinduism, Zen, Sufism, and Native American religion are mixed with humanistic psychology, Western occultism, and modern physics. New fads like crystals, rebirthing experiences, and sensory deprivation come and go. Individuals try various techniques (often called "psycho-technologies") and find that they do not provide what they promised. Instead of abandoning the New Age outlook, they try the next psychotechnology that promises health, enlightenment, greater brain power, or improved karma.

Many of the recommended experiences, from hallucinogenic drugs to yoga, Sufi dancing to breathing exercises, introduce the users to an altered state of consciousness (ASC). Marilyn Ferguson, author of the NAM "bible," wrote that "psychedelic drugs, how ever abused, had given a visionary experience of self-transcendence to a sufficient number of individuals, so that they might well determine the future of human development—not a Utopia, but a collectively altered state of consciousness."[1]

Elsewhere she catalogs ways to change consciousness:

"Deep inner shifts may occur in response to disciplined contemplation, grave illness, wilderness treks, peak emotions, creative effort, spiritual exercises, controlled breathing, techniques for 'inhibiting thought,' psychedelics, movement, isolation, music, hypnosis, meditation, reverie, and in the wake of intense intellectual struggle."[2] She connects yoga and monism in saying: "All souls are one. Each is a spark from the original soul, and this soul is inherent in all souls.... *Yoga* literally means 'union.'"[3]

Such expansions of consciousness tend to break down the boundaries between the individual and the world. One no longer feels isolated but united with everyone else, with the universe, and with divinity. A belief in the oneness of everything that exists is called *monism*, the third element in our definition. It is absolutely essential to keep in mind that New Agers do not come to their monistic belief through philosophical reasoning as much as through the experience of altered states of consciousness (ASCs). Since experience rather than theory grounds it, no one can deny that it happened. Other people merely reject the *interpretation* of the experience as proof that everything is one by denying that ASCs, instead of normal, shared, reasonable consciousness, are the norm for judging human experiences.

Once New Agers experience everything as a monist unity, they raise the question: what is the nature of the one reality of the universe? Most, though not all, New Agers believe that the universal One is God. Everything that exists is divine and shares in the divine nature. This is pantheism, the fourth element in our definition of NAM. New Age literature tends to focus more on the divine nature of human beings than on the divinity of animals or minerals. As an example, Shirley MacLaine writes, "Each soul is its own God. You must never worship anyone or anything other than self. For *you* are God. To love self is to love God."[4]

If everyone is God, then the human predicament is forgetfulness of our innate divinity. Remembering this inner divinity would solve the world's problems, as claimed by New Age educator Beverly Galyean: "Once we begin to see that we are all God, that we have the attributes of God, then I think the whole purpose of human life is to reown the Godlikeness within us; the perfect love, the perfect wisdom, the perfect understanding, the perfect intelligence. And when we do that, we create back to that old, that essential oneness which is consciousness."[5] No one would compete since all are equally God, and war would vanish as a result. Everyone would use divine power to cure illness, hunger, ecological disorders, and all other problems. These heady and very attractive promises lure many modern people who are otherwise anxious about the direction of the world and their own lives.

In general, the New Age fads are attempts to awaken the so-called divine energy within each person. When a particular method does not work, you search for the next, knowing that eventually you will find the one which will awaken your divinity. Besides, everyone is evolving into the divine realization, so each attempt at enlightenment is one more step to discovery of the true self. If one does not attain full enlightenment in this lifetime, the soul will return to new bodies in later lifetimes through reincarnation. Shirley MacLaine wrote that the soul "never dies and in fact cyclically reembodies itself in order to learn and grow while on the earth plane."[6] Everyone will return as often as is necessary to attain fulfillment.

This leads to the last element in our definition of NAM: millennialism. The movement gets it name from millennialism since they expect a new age to begin with the new millennium. Usually they identify it astrologically by calling it the Age of Aquarius. They believe that the last two thousand years were dominated by the sign Pisces (the fish), symbolizing Christianity. The new Age of Aquarius (the water-bearer) will be a time of peace and enlightenment. Ruth Montgomery's spirit guides say:

We are now at the threshold of the Aquarian Age, a period of enlightenment when men's minds will be opened to the reality of communication between the living and the so-called dead. This will be a vastly different period from the Piscean Age of the past two thousand years, which saw the persecution of Jesus and the division of his followers into militant sects who war on each other in the name of religion. The Guides insist that the shifting of the earth's axis in this new age should be welcomed rather than feared, because on the smoldering embers of our present civilization will arise a better one cleansed of strife and class hatreds.[7]

New Agers have no consensus about when the New Age begins. Dates range from the early twentieth century to the 1990s, to the year 2000, or even later. Some expect major natural catastrophes to occur in the late 1990s, like Ruth Montgomery's belief that the earth's axis will shift not to end the earth but to cleanse it of impurities.[8] Others, like Elizabeth Clare Prophet's Church Universal and Triumphant, expect a nuclear holocaust before peace begins. Most others predict a gentle evolution.

THE ROOTS OF THE NEW AGE MOVEMENT

NAM absorbs notions from various sources like Oriental religions, Western occultism, modern science, and humanistic psychology. Let readers beware: New Agers transform these sources, usually by popularizing them. It is not Hinduism and Buddhism, but Americanized versions of them which are taught. They include scientific opinions and psychological therapies compatible with the NAM worldview and offer simplified versions of them for general consumption. New Age beliefs are combined with the ideas of Carl

Rogers, Abraham Maslow, Carl Jung, and other pyscholo-gists. One's shadow personalities, archetypes, and need for freedom are taught in Catholic retreat houses and business seminars alike. Workshops promise greater creativity through contact with the goddess within and psychological wholeness through recognition of Myers-Briggs or ennea-gram personality types.

NAM uses the authority of these sources to back its claims. Oriental religions have the authority of antiquity, to which many New Agers appeal. Often the same appeal to antiquity is made for Western occult practices like astrology and Tarot cards. Modern science and psychology have tremendous authority in the Western world, so they are attractive to mod-ern readers. New Agers make a monistic claim that Hin-duism, Einsteinian physics, astrology, channeled spirits, and humanistic psychology are in complete harmony. This enchanting siren song charms people into joining the move-ment.

HOW THE NEW AGE BECAME A MOVEMENT

In the late 1950s, beatniks severely criticized the superfi-ciality of American society, but they did not convert the hearts of the majority. Most Americans were still basking in the extraordinary military success of World War II. Our dad-dies were heroes, the economy flourished, and everything looked wonderful. Why take the beatniks seriously?

Then came the 1960s. The young became disillusioned by the state of race relations in the land of the free. The shock of the race riots and the assassinations of key leaders frac-tured the nation further. The sour twist of the war in Vietnam and the soaring draft of young men tore America apart. Now the beatniks appeared to be prophets worthy of leading a burgeoning counterculture movement. They taught the young about the use of drugs, free sex, communal living, and the overturning of old cultural values. The youth subculture was more than willing to learn these lessons. Judaism and Christianity were seen as bourgeois and powerless to correct society. Other religions were examined, especially those from the mystical East. The counterculture of the 1960s became the nursery for the New Age Movement of the mid-1970s and the 1980s.

HOW SHOULD WE RESPOND?

I am confident that Catholicism has the resources to challenge NAM's worldview with God's alternatives. Our faith proclaims the good news that God loves us so much that he sent Jesus Christ, God incarnate and the Redeemer of the world's sin through his death and resurrection. It is a whole view of life, death, and the afterlife. The more we live our faith and understand it, the better we can discern what is true and false about NAM. Today the weak link is the lack of understanding of our faith. We need to shore up our knowledge of Scripture, church history, theology, and Christian morals. Yet this knowledge should never be disassociated from living the faith, making it strong in our personal lives.

Because our faith holds together so well, it can integrate science far better than NAM's creation of new mythologies. C.S. Lewis even proves the illogic of believing in science without faith in God in his book, *Miracles: A Preliminary Study*.[9] Furthermore, physicists and other scientists have serious criticisms of the often simplistic theories proposed by New Agers. Familiarity with science takes work, but it is worth the effort to be able to debunk astrology, the misuse of right-brain versus left-brain neurology, the existence of extraterrestrials, unidentified flying objects, and other speculations.

I bought into many ideas and practices which are now termed New Age during my college years—and I regret it.

Yet God's grace, good advice from Jesuit brothers, solid theological and philosophical reasoning, and help from scientist friends combined to lead me back to a lively faith in Christ. I invite readers involved in the New Age Movement to steer their way out of these deceptions as well. Catholics who are not involved in it can learn how to lead others out of its traps. See my last chapter for some tips. We cannot cover every possible aspect of the New Age for Catholics in this book, but we can learn from my mistakes and get a start by identifying and understanding some key points of NAM's teachings.

First, let's explore in Chapter One why a young Jesuit seminarian like myself began to dabble in what are now considered New Age ideas and practices back in the late 1960s and the early 1970s. How did I get involved in these ideas and practices? Why were they attractive—at least at first?

ONE

Keeping up with the Gurus

AFTER ONE YEAR OF COLLEGE I entered the Jesuit novitiate at Milford, Ohio, in August 1968, days before the riots at the Democratic Convention in my hometown of Chicago. Two-thirds of the novices left Milford that year and we closed the large operation down. Most of us novices went to Holy Family parish on Chicago's Near West Side for a hot summer of social work in the inner city. I worked with a Mexican street gang called Satan's Disciples, while the others worked in the Black community across the street. Too young at age twenty to appreciate the high risk of getting in the middle of gang fights to try and stop them, I loved the work and stayed on for the whole year. Only after I witnessed the murder of my good friend, Jimmy "Baby-face" Valadez, did I realize that moving away was my only safe recourse.

INITIAL PHILOSOPHICAL BELIEFS

My first contacts with ideas and practices now associated with the New Age Movement came as my two-year novitiate ended and philosophy studies began. After Jimmy's murder in May of 1970, I hid out at Loyola University for the rest of the summer. While there, my master of novices suggested that I take an introductory class in philosophy to prepare for the church's and Jesuit's required program of philosophy studies. Already angry about moving out of pastoral work with street gangs, I hated the idea of jumping through a church-imposed hoop. What good could philosophy be? It did not have any practical purpose! My expectations of philosophy were vague, except that it would certainly be dull and useless.

To my amazement, Dr. Robert Barry's *Philosophy of Man* course was exciting from the very first lecture. He questioned our assumptions about culture, the relationships between men and women, and human interaction with the environment. He suggested that humans can create their own environment, as seen in the change from a rural society dependent on the rhythms of nature to an urban society wherein people established their own daily rhythms. People liberated themselves from natural rhythms like nocturnal darkness through electricity, or the change of season through heating and air conditioning. Men did not need to dominate women and the whole of culture as they did on the farm because urban folk used more of their brain than their brawn for survival.

People not only have the power to create their own world, but they need to create something in order to know it truly. Plato's dictum, "An unexamined life is not worth living," was the key principle in Dr. Barry's course.

His lectures examined the meaning of God, time, objectivity, and human experience. He did not offer answers but raised questions I had never considered before. These new considerations fostered a desire to reflect on human existence. This resulted in my registering as an undergraduate majoring in philosophy when I enrolled at the University of Detroit that fall.

Some of Dr. Barry's issues affected me at a time of decision regarding my future ministry plans. As a second-year novice from 1969 to 1970, I did community organizing at Holy Family parish. Issues of social justice for the poor and race relations dominated my future plans as a Jesuit. I even had permission to remain in Chicago, so I could integrate my college and philosophy studies with a career in community organizing. The murder of my friend, Jimmy "Baby-face" Valadez, changed all that. His murderers came looking for me, the sole witness to their crime, so I could no longer safely work in the parish. I felt more than incompetent at this work, and blamed myself for mishandling the situation so badly that Jimmy got killed. Waves of anger, even rage, passed over me because I had to study in Detroit, with the likelihood of having to teach in a high school someday instead of doing parish work. My plans to change the world through community organizing and social work were changing, and I hated it.

Some of the books on Dr. Barry's recommended reading list helped me to rethink my plans for social justice work and community organizing. Theodore Roszak's *Making of a Counterculture* identified two main styles within the counterculture of the American youth in the late 1960s. One was politically interested in demanding social justice, while the other sought spiritual development. Since my senior year in high school, I had identified with the first style. After the devastating experience of witnessing murder, I wondered whether I should change my orientation and let the spiritual dominate my attention. The very day I started reading Roszak I also picked up Hermann Hesse's *Siddhartha*, a novel about Buddha attaining spiritual enlightenment. My journal for July 7, 1970 shows that I desired Siddhartha's discovery of peace and unity in all things.

At Mass that evening the insight came that all things—history, peoples, and creation—are made one in Christ. Following his commands would give me the inner peace I craved. For two years the ideas of the counterculture and the faith of Christianity vied for my complete loyalty. I wanted to remain a good Catholic and a Jesuit, but I felt strongly attracted to non-Christian ideas as well. I hoped to integrate them someday.

A FULLER WORLDVIEW

Another highly influential book on that list was R. Buckminster Fuller's *Utopia or Oblivion*. Fuller taught that humans had to make a fundamental choice before the turn of the twenty-first century: either completely destroy the planet through nuclear war, or create a utopia on earth for everyone. He was determined to construct a utopia through a design-science revolution. His plan started with a World Game plan, modeled on the computerized war games of American armed forces, though redirected to world peace. Armies, navies, and air forces were ingenious at designing lighter, faster inventions to deliver their weapons systems. Why not design inventions for living at ever higher standards with fewer resources, the way military inventors do for weaponry? These ideas appealed to me immensely, especially since they did not require political parties or armies to enforce them. I could continue my social justice concerns through redesigning the environment, without embarking incompetently into politics.

I could hardly believe my ears when I heard that the first person to hold the "R. Buckminster Fuller Chair" of architecture at the University of Detroit was my new hero— "Bucky" Fuller himself. He was scheduled to lecture every month at the university as part of a year-long, fourteen-credit-hour course called World Game. Even though the Jesuit collegians' dean, Fr. Ed Miller, told me not to take this course, I endorsed my own registration permission and signed up anyway. Educators of the time strongly suggested that students who choose their own program of studies do better than those who follow an imposed agenda. I decided to learn more by that theory of studies instead of being obedient to my superiors.

A group of architecture students built a geodesic dome, one of Fuller's most famous inventions, on our campus. They taught the World Game course when Fuller was out of town, which was most of the time. All of them, it turned out, were practicing Bahais. Their prophet, Baha Ullah, taught that all of the great religious leaders in history were reincarnations of one and the same entity. Buddha, Moses, Jesus, and Mohammed appeared in different eras to manifest an evolving doctrine of God and morality. The last incarnation of this entity was Baha Ullah himself, teaching that all religions were in fact one.

They did not teach the World Game class about their one religion doctrine, but it was frequently brought up among the students most devoted to the course. They explained their religion and a number of times asked me to convert from Catholicism to Bahaism. Obviously, belief in a one-world syncretistic religion revealed by a Persian prophet supported their global view of economics, ecology, and politics.

The World Game classes studied ecology, computerization, transportation, food distribution, and other global issues that came to mind. The students ranged from long-haired freaks to crew-cut engineering students. Whether brewing mu tea for each other or teaching computer languages, most of them shared the kind of good feelings one associates with counterculture activities.

During my two years of undergraduate studies at the University of Detroit, I read all of Fuller's books and integrated his thought in my philosophy papers. I chose topics like Buckminster Fuller's theory of politics, his view of the development of technology throughout history, science, and even theology. Under his tutelage I rejected political solutions to the world's problems in favor of scientific and engineering improvements. Since politicians do not create new resources but merely theorize ways to distribute what already exists, avoid them and use science to increase the world's wealth. In addition, the earth is a whole ecological system without real borders. The solutions to its problems must inevitably unite all people into a one-world government to rehabilitate the pollution of the oceans, air, and other ecological issues that transcend national borders.

MY FAITH AND TEILHARD

The World Game course ran in the academic year 1970-1971, changing my ideas about politics and the solutions to the world's problems. My Catholic faith was strong: attending Mass daily in the Jesuit community, meditating on the Gospels for an hour each day, and participating in prayer groups with other Jesuit collegians. Sometimes I prayed for the whole world, asking God to bring about the utopia Bucky Fuller described in his lectures. Sometimes I wondered how my new worldview corresponded to my faith. My friends in the World Game course found theological support for their global perspective by adhering to Bahaism, but I wanted a Catholic theological perspective.

Like many Catholics of that time, I read the books of Pierre Teilhard de Chardin, a French Jesuit paleontologist (1881-1955). In the fall of 1971, Fr. Thomas Charbeneau, S.J., offered a graduate seminar on Teilhard, teaching his evolutionary worldview and exploring its ramifications for the Christian message. This was the theology I was looking for.

Teilhard was a paleontologist; he studied the history of life forms through their fossil remains. This training formed his thought about the world, life, and human beings in terms of millions of years. The evolution of life and consciousness was basic to his belief. Teilhard applied these ideas of evolution to his philosophy of life and theology, creating a new synthesis.

On the basis of reason alone, Teilhard believed that the dispersed and disorganized mass of energy and atoms in the universe were evolving to a convergence on God. From science he knew that each unit of the cosmos, from the smallest hydrogen atom to the most complex organism, contained a center that kept it from dissipating. Such atomic, planetary, or organic centers represented a form of consciousness, primitive in the elements and most complex in human beings. This idea led Teilhard to deny the dichotomy between matter and spirit, claiming that spirit is hypercentered matter, and that all matter is centered and therefore psychic.

His studies of the development of life forms on earth led him to believe in "orthogenesis." This term refers to purpose within the universe as every element, molecule, and species develops in a preordained path. He did not completely reject the role of chance and natural selection dominating evolutionary theories of his day. But he did believe that nature constantly sought increasing complexity and thereby greater spirit, groping for progressive development.

For Teilhard this drive to increasingly complex organization comes from within each unit, whether atomic or organic, and it moves toward a final goal of total spiritualization in what he calls an Omega Point or God. He espoused the idea of various spheres on the planet: the biosphere refers to the layer of life in and above the soil; and the noosphere means the layer of human thought, invention, and progress on the earth. Both are evolutionary developments which will result in the Omega Point of the ideal society and perfected homo sapiens, completely at one with God. One must remember that Teilhard talks this way in his scientific and philosophical mode, especially in the book *Phenomenon of Man*, so that he can convince his non-believing colleagues in the sciences.

Teilhard the believing Catholic writes differently, no longer depending on reason alone but making an act of faith in Christ and the gospel. He places his concerns about the relationship of spirit and matter at the center of his approach to Christianity. In his theologically oriented books, he identifies Christ as the Omega Point because Christ is God made flesh, the truly divine entering real matter. Therefore, everything is evolving toward Christ since he is the force within the material world that drives it forward to perfection.

While humans cannot love progress or the universe, they can love Christ, who gives the universe its center. When people join the church they become members of the Mystical Body of Christ, which Teilhard compares to a new phylum (new division) in the evolution of the world. The source of energy for this new phylum is the love that Christ gives it. Christians who respond to this love perform the actions that push evolution and progress forward to the *Parousia*, the coming of Christ in his full glory. Teilhard even calls this growth toward the *Pleroma* (Greek word for fullness) "Christogenesis." In the *Pleroma* everything will be united to God through Christ, and everyone will be united to one another through him. Yet Teilhard never understood this in a pantheistic way, wherein people lose their individuality by absorption into divinity. For Teilhard, true unity with Christ makes us more distinctive individuals, based on his principle, "Unity differentiates."

My understanding of Teilhard gave a new thrust to my World Game vision of life. Of course, I wrote my paper for Fr. Charbeneau's course on the relationship between Buckminster Fuller and Teilhard de Chardin. It highlighted their beliefs in evolutionary movement toward progress and utopia on earth. Bucky, a Unitarian, believed that God is a "verb" rather than a noun, and that a general love in the universe would bring humanity forward. Teilhard had faith in Christ Jesus as the center and goal of evolution, loving the cosmos, evoking love from it, and offering eternal life. Teilhard firmly believed in the incarnation of God in the historical Jesus Christ, his bodily resurrection and ascension, the church and the sacraments, especially the Mass. His faith gave me intellectual permission to continue believing in these key doctrines of our religion, so I was very glad to take Teilhard as my theologian.

Like so many people who adopt a hero, I was partially blind to some of Teilhard's deficiencies. He admitted that the major stumbling block to his evolutionary model of the universe was the doctrine of original sin. Was this merely a logical explanation of the presence of tremendous evil in the world as conceived in a static view of creation? Did humans need the incarnation of God in Christ to redeem them from sin more than they needed God to enter evolution from within? Teilhard saw the Fall not as a single act but as the physical and spiritual entropy, that is, disintegration and loss of center, which is inherent in the world. This changed the doctrine of original sin from disobedience of God to a natural weakness innate to the universe. Christ's incarnation was therefore meant primarily to advance evolution, correcting dissipation and entropy in nature, and leading the cosmos into the *Pleroma*.

The church, however, has consistently taught that the first humans rebelled against God's command and committed sin. This sin is passed on to all other humans: "Therefore, through one man sin entered the world and through sin death, so that death has passed to all humans since all have sinned" (Rom 5:12-21). The only exceptions are Jesus Christ, "who did not know sin" (1 Cor 5:21; see also Heb 4:15), and his Mother, the Blessed Virgin Mary, who is "the most blessed of all women" (Lk 1:42) and who was preserved from original sin by a special grace. Teilhard did not have a way of integrating this doctrine into his theory of evolution because it was more closely tied in with his scientific view than with his faith.

Another weakness in Teilhard is his neglect of the doctrine of God. He rarely speaks about the Blessed Trinity. He concentrates on Christ because he is concerned with the relationship between God, matter, and evolution. His writings are unclear about the nature of God. Is God distinct from the process of evolution, or is he the result of it? Does God's actual being evolve along with the universe? By saying that the body of Christ is a new phylum in creation in a process of "Christogenesis," he indicates that Christ is evolving because of his intimate union with matter through the incarnation. Does this mean that the Father and the Holy Spirit are evolving too? Does Teilhard mean to say that Christ's divine nature is evolving?

Teilhard carelessly ignored these problems, unwittingly setting theological traps for some of his fans. People who are not well grounded in Scripture and church teaching about the nature of God and the Trinity can easily slip into pantheism when reading Teilhard. I do not believe that he held pantheism. In fact, he criticized Hinduism precisely for holding that creation is God. But his neglect of the doctrine of God has frequently led New Agers to appropriate his ideas, especially from the *Phenomenon of Man*, as support for pantheism from a Catholic perspective.

The church does not define what God and the Trinity mean as much as it lays out the tensions within revelation that must be held by the faithful. These tensions—like the oneness of God and the Three Persons, the incarnation of the Second Person in human flesh—make the teachings mysteries that invite us to be expanded by the infinite and eternal God. He will not be limited by our very reasonable but shortsighted ideas that he evolves, is equated with creation, or has no community of persons from all eternity. Studying and meditating on more solid material from church teaching on the nature of God and the Blessed Trinity will not remove the mystery from our religion, but preserve it.

I am grateful that my reading of Teilhard helped me to remain faithful to many key doctrines of our faith. When even Catholic theologians denied the virgin birth or the bodily resurrection of Jesus Christ, I could look to as "liberal" a support as Teilhard for permission to believe these things. However, as the years moved on and I learned more theology, I came to admit Teilhard's theological weaknesses and limits. I shifted away from his thought to a doctrinal position capable of including a fuller understanding of teachings on sacred revelation about God, Christ, the future of the world, sin, and redemption.

In many ways we young Jesuits differed from our fellow college students, especially in our commitment to God, the church, and organized religion. Our classmates drifted away from Christian sexual morality, used drugs, and got interested in Oriental religions. To better understand and someday evangelize my counterculture friends, I decided to study Oriental religions at the University of Detroit.

My professor was Dr. T.K. Venkateswaran, an Indian from Madras who was one of the finest gentlemen I have ever met in my life. At times class was difficult to interpret because he had a strong accent, but his kindness and intelligence always came through. I appreciated the ways he explained the various religions of the East and connected them to Christian ideas. At the same time, he sobered most of my romanticism about Hindu, Buddhist, and Taoist theologies.

After that introductory course, I continued to research the history of Hinduism and exposed elements which most Westerners (even many New Agers) would find unacceptable. A short examination of these teachings may help us to bring New Agers to a more serious reassessment of their claims and romance with the Orient.

A REVEALING STUDY OF HINDUISM

Many Westerners think of Hinduism as a unified, monolithic religion ready-made in the far distant past. In fact, it developed over many centuries into widely diverse forms. The Dravidians, the original people of the Indian sub-continent, apparently worshiped a mother goddess. Third millennium B.C. archaeological evidence from their civilization depicts individuals seated in the famous cross-legged lotus position.

Around 2000 B.C. a light-skinned Aryan people from Persia conquered the darker Dravidians and imposed a new religion and social system upon them. The victors' god of war became the chief deity, though the Dravidian gods gradually worked their way back into the religious system. The Aryans imposed a new social structure in which their priests formed the *Brahmin* caste, and the soldiers and nobles became the *Kshatriya* caste. The dark skinned Dravidians were considered "untouchables," incarnate demons unworthy of paradise after death. The *Brahmins'* control of religion kept them at the top of society. They composed the earliest Hindu literature, the *Rig Veda*, containing hymns, poems, and rituals of sacrifice between 1500 and 1000 B.C. The strong focus on rituals and sacrifices also served to exclude the untouchables.

Around the ninth century B.C. a countermovement of yogis and non-*Brahmin* philosophers rose to popular strength in India. Though many *Brahmins* opposed them, these religious leaders freed the religion from rituals and taught the people ways to meditate and experience the gods apart from the priests. Their teachings were written in the *Upanishads*, additions to the *Vedas* composed from the ninth century B.C. to the first century A.D. These yogis did *not* share a common faith: some were atheists, some were agnostics, and others believed in one or more divinities. They were more interested in religious experience, making doctrine relatively unimportant.

Many of the later schools of yoga trace themselves to the *Upanishadic* period or are inspired by that development. Dr. Venkateswaran described the Hindu concept of deity from the *Upanishadic* period as a type of hierarchy. For the yogis the ultimate reality and truth is *Brahman*. *Brahman* does not have human characteristics but is the impersonal ground of all being, of all that is. *Brahman* is in the deepest self of every person, which the yogis call the *Atman*.

Some yogis claim that *Atman* and *Brahman* are one, and they define the human as "Thou art That," you are *Brahman*. Therefore the goal of *Upanishadic* religion is the discovery of *Brahman* within oneself. The Theosophical tradition of Madame Blavatsky, with some roots in Hinduism, brought this idea to the West in the nineteenth century. They urged devotees to find that "I AM" within themselves and realize that they are divine.

Many New Age teachers and cults, sometimes under the influence of Hindu missionaries, established enlightenment or the realization of inner divinity as their goal. Their techniques or "psycho-technologies" are merely aids in attaining the consciousness of oneness with divinity (monism) and the divinity of all beings, especially people (pantheism).

Upanishadic Hinduism had a variety of its own techniques for coming to awareness, which were often called "yoga," which means "yoke," since it yokes or joins one to divinity. The four main types of yoga are: knowledge or *jnana yoga*; love and devotion or *bhakti yoga*; work and effort or *karma yoga*; and psychological and physical exercises and meditation or *raja yoga*. Most New Agers are familiar with *raja yoga*, typically seen in exercises like sitting cross-legged in the "lotus position," or standing on one's head or shoulders, or in exercises requiring the flexibility of a contortionist. Remember, Hindus did not devise these exercises for athletic limbering or muscle building. All were meant to lead the practitioner to enlightenment and the awareness of his or her inner divinity.

Two other distinctive Hindu doctrines, *karma* and *samsara*, deal with sin and limitation in life. Hinduism teaches that there are four goals in life: pleasure, sex, and aesthetic joy (*kama*); worldly success, material gain, social and political fulfillment (*artha*); duty, righteousness, and law (*dharma*); and liberation in the religious and spiritual realms of life (*mukti* or *moksha*). However, as all religions and philosophies observe, people do not usually reach their goals or live in total bliss. Some people even choose to break the moral law and thwart the attainment of their goals. In Hinduism these failures are seen either as sin or as imperfections in nature and human personality.

This does not mean humans are viewed as inherently evil in Hinduism. In fact, good and evil are not moral absolutes at war with each other. Rather, people must take responsibility for sins and imperfections and work to change them. If one fails to change in the present lifetime and realize the *atman* or inner self, the soul will transmigrate to a different body in another lifetime. This transmigration is called *sam - sara*. The law of cause and effect—*karma*—determines what kind of body you will enter next. If a person morally improves then the next body will be at a higher level; sin and failure will cause trouble in the next incarnation. The scale of values for the incarnations places the insects and most animals at the lower end of the transmigration scale.

A sinful human will return as an animal, and a bad animal will keep going lower down the scale of life until that individual learns to become good. On this scale, the female is lower than the male, so a bad man may return as a woman, while a good woman may move up to become a man in the next lifetime. There is also a hierarchy among the castes, with the *Brahmins* (originally the priests of the conquering Aryans) at the top. Good people can reincarnate in future lifetimes in higher castes.

The goal is that eventually a highly developed soul may return as a *Brahmin* cow or bull, which is the most advanced state on earth. After life as a *Brahmin* bull a soul can spin out of the cycle of reincarnation and reach the great goal of total union with *Brahman*. At that point the individual soul will disintegrate into the vastness of *Brahman* like a drop of water that loses its individuality when it merges with the ocean.

The importance in knowing Hindu beliefs is to discern its difference from New Age teachings on reincarnation and *karma*. Some of the Hindu missionaries to the West redefined good and evil because of their own notions of pantheism. The late Shree Rajneesh said, "My *ashram* makes no difference between the demonic and the divine."[1] Swami Vivekananda taught, "Good and evil are one and the same," and "The Murderer, too, is God."[2]

Typical of New Age beliefs about *karma* is Shirley MacLaine: "*Karma*, that is, cause and effect, came into being as a path, a means, a method, to eventually eliminate the artificial concepts of good and evil."[3] "The learning process which is *karma* is not punitive. It simply follows the laws of science— for every effect there was a cause—so that in the human condition, *karma* translated as experience *all* experience."[4] MacLaine begins by making the law of *karma* an amoral principle that will eventually make all ideas of good and evil disappear. Then she writes:

> ... the purpose of life was to work one's way back to the Divine Source of which we were all a part. And the karmic events that we encountered along the way were only to be experienced and understood—never to be judged. Each of the great books had warned *against* judgment, *against* the moral trap of good versus evil. The laws of cause and effect were the underlying principles of all their teachings: *Judge and you will be judged; hurt and you will be hurt; love and you will be loved; give and you will be given to.* They taught that circumstances never mattered. They were only the field on which our truth was played out. (emphasis mine)[5]

Since good and evil do not exist, judgment of behavior is impossible: the norms for judgment do not exist. Notice, too, how MacLaine misquotes Luke 6:36-38—inaccurately and out of context. Truly Jesus Christ commanded us not to judge one another in this life, but he never eliminated judgment as a principle, let alone good and evil. He himself will return at the end of time to judge every person, as he proclaims in Matthew 24:29-35; 25:31-46, as well as in the parables of the kingdom (Mt 13), and the Book of Revelation, just to cite a few texts.

New Agers falsify the Hindu notion about reincarnation by rejecting the hierarchy of value inherent in each incarnation. Instead of teaching that people go up and down the scale of life, New Agers prefer to teach that every incarnation is a learning experience chosen for its educational value before one incarnates. Again, MacLaine is typical of New Agers on this point:

> The concrete difference between the karmic spiritual perspective and the earth plane, "prove it," materialistic perspective was self-responsibility. When we realized *we* were responsible for everything that happened to us, we could get on with living in a positive and contributive way. And that went for everything, whether it was a love affair, a death, a lost job, or a disease. *We* choose to have these experiences in order to learn from them—and to me, that is what life is about: learning. Learning and enjoying the knowledge that life is all about lessons.[6]

MacLaine, Ruth Montgomery, and others believe that after each life, a person chooses what kind of life he or she will enter next—will I be rich? will I be smart? will I be male or female, healthy or sick? Que sera, sera! That is why MacLaine states that we are "responsible for everything that happened to us"—we chose it before we were born. People choose to have cancer, alcoholism, or other problems in order to learn the lessons these experiences can teach. They go off to another life, another experience, and its lessons. Notice how radically different this is from the Hindu idea of reincarnation. MacLaine would never believe that she is a woman because she had been a bad man before. She does not even believe that bad or good exist!

Back to Hinduism.

Brahman, the ground of all being present in all beings, can be too impersonal and even dull for the average human being to love or adore. Therefore, *Brahman* became manifest in male and female divinities—over three hundred thirty million of them. The chief gods include Ishwara the father god who reveals *Brahman* as a person who has a will and who loves. On a par with Ishwara is Shakti Devi, a mother goddess found in the earliest *Rig Vedas*, who represents the personal approach to *Brahman*. Three gods exhibit Ishwara's specialized functions: Brahma is the creator function; Vishnu is the protector; and Shiva is the destroyer who corrects all imbalances in the universe. Their three divine wives manifest Shakti: Sarasvati is the goddess of learning; Lakshmi is the goddess of prosperity; and Parvati represents energy or powers.

One would be mistaken to understand the Hindu deities as a trinity, since that Christian term means "one God and Three Persons." Rather, the chief gods personalize functions of the father deity, Ishwara, as a triad of male and female pairs. To redefine the Hindu gods as a trinity, as Elizabeth Clare Prophet does (see Chapter Seven), misrepresents both Hinduism and Christianity.

After these deities of the classical *Upanishads* come the three hundred thirty million gods and goddesses worshiped in the popular religion of the temples and villages. Typically, the elite or religiously well-educated believe the purer forms of Hinduism. But since Hinduism is an experiential and philosophical faith, most believers do not feel the need to force other people to comply with an authoritative orthodoxy. People can choose the divinities or style of yoga that best manifests the truth of *Brahman* in their own *atman* or innermost self.

Already one can see that Hinduism is no ancient monolith of a religion, but rather a very diverse and evolving faith without systematization. This complex diversity in Hinduism also appears in its philosophical developments. Three later Hindu scholars developed diverging philosophies from the earlier *Vedanta*, a seventh-century B.C. system of commentary on the *Vedas* found in written *Sutras*.

The first and most influential of the later exegetes was Shankara, who lived around A.D. 800. He based his philosophy on the *Upanishads*, the *Brahma Sutra*, and the more popular *Bhagavad Gita* written in the third century B.C. His approach was to bring this diverse and sometimes contradictory literature into a unified perspective, which fit his monistic view of reality. He taught that the material world was an illusion *(maya)* relative to the spiritual, since only the latter was truly important. He introduced genuine pantheism into the Hindu interpretation of the *Upanishads* by holding that behind the illusion of matter is the reality of the one godhead, *Brahman*. Everything is *Brahman*; the differences visible in the physical world are the mirage of *maya* which is relative reality.

Though at first someone may need to worship an individual personal god, eventually everyone will realize that the *atman*, the essence of each person, is god. Behind the illusion of the physical person stands the reality that each person is essentially *Brahman*. Shankara taught that the way to realize the oneness of all in the divine being was through mystical enlightenment in which the person experiences divinity within and oneness with *Brahman*. Hardly any other individual influenced Hinduism as much as Shankara, so that most of the New Age ideas about Hinduism can be traced to his interpretations.

The second great teacher was Ramaniya, an eleventh-century commentator on the *Vedantas*. He believed that the supreme is personal and includes the universe, embracing both the inorganic and the human, in its body. The material corresponds to the spiritual as its direct manifestation. Therefore, the way to enlightenment is through loving and devoted human effort in conjunction with the deity's work. His image for the divine-human cooperation is that of a baby monkey with its mother. The mother leaps from tree to tree, but the baby travels with the mother only by clinging firmly to her. The deity will save humans only if they cling to him or her.

The third philosopher is the twelfth-century Madhva, who gave a more theological than philosophical commentary on the *Vedantas*. He believed that human souls were completely plural, fully distinct from one another and from God. Madhva did not teach either monism or pantheism.

The purpose of this overview is to show that Hinduism is a complex religion that has developed in many different directions over the past thirty-five centuries. In fact, this overview shows only part of Hinduism's diversity. A multitude of developments and differences remain for the avid student to explore. The reader can keep these ideas in mind when reading the New Agers' views of Hinduism to detect the many ways they pick and choose certain doctrines, transforming them into a highly Americanized form of Hinduism. They may like their version better than the Indian forms, but honesty requires an admission of how much they have westernized Hinduism.

TWO

In the Shadow of Dr. Jung

WITNESSING THE MURDER of my friend Jimmy "Baby-face" Valadez led to frequent nightmares. Nearly every night enemies chased and attacked me in urban alleys and streets, making me afraid to sleep. The light was always lit in my bedroom, and sometimes a friend would sit in a chair in my room until I fell asleep. Sleep terrified me. To overcome the nightmares' effects, sometimes I wrote the dreams in a journal. This led to writing my dreams, even when no one hunted me down. It awakened an interest in my whole dream or unconscious life.

Another step inward was taken when fellow Jesuit seminarians and other university students met in a meditation group each week. Each of us took turns leading meditations: sometimes reading Scripture and then listening to Christian music. Jim, a young Jesuit, liked to experiment with imagination exercises. Lowering the lights, he asked us to breathe deeply for a while, and then guided us into our subconscious through imaginary trips. The experience was relaxing and sometimes prayerful if we pictured Jesus, but we did not always include Christ in this exercise because Jim's goal was to kindle our imagination as a *preparation* for prayer.

A third opening to my inner world was when Jim introduced me to smoking hashish and marijuana. As with many of my contemporaries, this brought me bliss and intensified awareness of sense or mental experience. My explorations in drugs were limited, but spread out over a year and a half. While I told myself that these were just experiments to explore cannabis' possibilities, I now admit enjoying its pleasures. Although my superiors forbade me to smoke dope, I occasionally continued to do so. I added disobedience to the vice of drug abuse. I smoked with college friends, went to Disney's *Fantasia* stoned, and meditated while high. This was part of the countercultural scene of college life in the early 1970s, and I increasingly wanted to be part of it. I justified smoking marijuana by contrasting its benefits with the worse effects of alcohol. If older Americans could drink, why couldn't younger people smoke marijuana? Permitting one and forbidding the other seemed hypocritical.

Dream-work, meditation and imagination exercises, and experiments with hallucinogens triggered a need for interior life. I was seeking understanding (to paraphrase the traditional dictum, *fides quaerens intellectum*: "faith seeking understanding"). Carl Gustave Jung's depth psychology provided the creative framework to interpret the images emerging from my psyche.

FIRST CONTACT WITH JUNG

The once-dreaded philosophy studies proved to be my best academic effort ever. My superiors thought I needed intellectual stretching so they sent Dick Weber, a novitiate classmate, and me to Bronx, New York. We enrolled for a summer of intense philosophy studies at Fordham University and lived in an off-campus apartment of Jesuit graduate students for the summer. A three-week intensive course on Heidegger's existentialism was followed by an easier, but slow-moving class on ethics. For mental stimulation I picked up a volume belonging to a psychology graduate student. It was Fr. Robert Sears' copy of *Man and His Symbols*, an introduction to C.G. Jung's thought. The book was beautifully illustrated, and Jung's ideas were exhilarating. He was the first psychoanalyst to teach the importance of spiritual experience. Sigmund Freud had reduced everything but his cigars to a sexual significance, especially in culture and religion. However, Carl Jung, his one-time friend, disciple, and heir apparent, believed that dreams and the subconscious life were integral to spiritual experiences. This pioneer psychiatrist accepted religion as a serious aid for mental health and used religious symbolism for therapeutic techniques like dream interpretation.

With a scientific perspective, he seemed to consider the Christian faith more than gullible superstition or purely subjective experience. He studied the symbolism of the Mass, the role of the Virgin Mary, the Spiritual Exercises of St. Ignatius Loyola, and other Catholic beliefs and practices. His serious scientific treatment of Catholicism made it seem more worthy of belief.

Jung also sparked my enthusiasm with his insights into individuation (the process of becoming psychologically whole). He observed that within each person many opposites exist. The unconscious tries to bring these opposites together to create psychological wholeness in each person. Dreams form symbols for the conscious ego, the part of our personality which acts in everyday life.

In dreams, males symbolize a man's conscious life and females symbolize a woman's conscious life. The unconscious has its symbols, too: the female (which Jung calls the *anima*) is a symbol for a man's unconscious; and the male (called *animus*), for a woman's unconscious. There are shadow figures representing unknown, dark, unassimilated aspects brought forth by the unconscious for recognition and integration by the conscious self. Using these and many other symbols of Jung's studies on patients, mythology, and

Christian symbolism, I interpreted my dreams, fantasies, and fears. I read Jung's books, took courses in seminary, and analyzed myself for years.

Enthusiasm for Jung's openness to Christianity prevented me from criticizing his perspective on religion. Nevertheless, he included occult practices in his scientific research and therapy, like astrology and the Chinese technique of divination called the *I Ching*. His objective, scientific authority removed any qualms about transgressing Catholic prohibitions against the occult, so I studied astrology. According to Jung, it could be scientific and therapeutic! Furthermore, I was oblivious to Jung's teaching about God, Jesus Christ, Christianity, the church, and the afterlife. Since many Christians today take a Jungian perspective on spirituality and teach others to do the same, it would be helpful to examine his theology here. Later I will treat my involvement with astrology.

BASIC JUNGIAN CONCEPTS

Like Freud, Jung believed that people live both on the conscious level (where we are aware of what we know) and on the unconscious level (where the elements of our interior life are unknown). Dreams are a fundamental way for the unconscious to communicate with the conscious. The predicament is that the unconscious uses symbolic language which is difficult for the conscious mind to interpret. Therefore, dream work can be demanding and perplexing. However, Jung believed that if the conscious mind ignored the messages of the unconscious, psychological disturbances could result, especially in later life. Wholeness is possible only when a person integrates the negative "shadow" and dark side with the more acceptable, conscious ego. Consequently, the need to understand the unconscious is serious.

Besides the personal unconscious, Jung also believed in a

collective unconscious that belongs to the whole human race. He came to this conclusion on the basis of reading the myths and fairy tales of many nations, along with gnostic and alchemical writings from Europe, and the experience of psychotherapy.

He noticed the remarkable similarity between the dreams of his patients and the images of the myths, even when it was impossible for the patient to have consciously known the myth. He inferred from these experiences that a storehouse of unconscious images belongs to the whole human race. He hypothesized that these images may be passed on through heredity, like human instincts. The images can arise within any particular person unbidden and without prior conscious knowledge of it.

Jung named these powerful images of the collective unconscious "archetypes." They are forms or ideas which have no content until they become conscious, but which manifest themselves spontaneously and autonomously as the structure of a dream.

My qualms about Jung's approach began when I realized that he interpreted Christian doctrines from a mythic perspective and set them in the larger pattern of archetypes of the collective unconscious. I wanted to believe that Christianity was historically and objectively true, not just a myth, no matter how cleverly myth was redefined. By entering the Jesuits and taking my vows, I had given my life to Jesus Christ. If Christ were just an archetype, I do not think I could have remained a Jesuit. Myths and archetypes are too hollow for me to give up having a wife, children, and home.

A classic example is his *mandala* archetype and Christian symbols and doctrines. The *mandala*, according to Jung, is a "magic circle" represented by either a circle, a square, or other arrangements of four items. He claimed that it symbolized the totality of the self, the centered self in which psychological chaos finds order and harmony. Jung identified Christian symbols of Jesus surrounded by the four evangelists, the cross, or the stained-glass rose windows of the Gothic churches.

Much more controversial is his *mandala* interpretation of the Blessed Trinity. Since Scripture and the church teach that there are three persons in one God, the *mandala's* demand for fourness is missing. Jung therefore interpreted the 1950 declaration of the doctrine of the assumption of the Blessed Virgin Mary as the Catholic church's recognition that Mary had become the fourth person of the Trinity. This not only forms a quaternity necessary for a *mandala,* but adds the necessary feminine element. Once, when I was in graduate school, some Protestant seminarians sympathetic to Jung's ideas asked me if the Catholic church really did make Mary the fourth person of the Trinity!

It is one thing to interpret medieval Catholic art as *mandalas* since that would be merely one critic's explanation of artistic representation. It is entirely different to interpret Pope Pius XII's definition of the assumption of the Blessed Virgin Mary as the addition of a person to the Trinity! The Catholic church does not have the authority to add anybody to God. We can only submit to the truths God reveals about himself.

Through Jesus Christ, the Son of God, God revealed that there are three persons in one God. This revelation began at Jesus' conception, when the Father sent the Holy Spirit to overshadow the Virgin Mary so that God the Son might be conceived in her womb. The Trinity was again revealed at Jesus' baptism in the Jordan River. God the Father said, "You are my beloved Son in whom I am well pleased," and the Holy Spirit hovered over Jesus, God the Son, made flesh. When Jesus taught the apostles about baptism, he instructed them to baptize all nations "in the name of the Father and of the Son and of the Holy Spirit." The "name" is singular but the persons are three. These and many other parts of the New Testament are the authority for the church's teaching on the Blessed Trinity. It is not the church's creation, so the church cannot change it.

I could not commit myself to the gospel of Christ if it were merely the product of the unconscious—personal or collective. Rather, Christ Jesus left a faith and a church to his apostles, for which Christians have lived and given their lives. Jung has completely missed the mark by interpreting the declaration of the doctrine of Blessed Mary's assumption into heaven as an addition of the feminine to the Godhead.

Jung and Christian Doctrine. A careful reading of Jung's autobiography helped me understand the three basic concepts underlying his interpretation of the Trinity and other Christian doctrines. The first two concepts, faith and personal experience, should be treated in tandem.

First, Jung saw faith as the blind acceptance of doctrines, blocking the believer from true wholeness. "The arch sin of faith, it seemed to me, was that it forestalled experience."[1] In his view faith was a sin! He even tried a serious study of Christian doctrine, but it could not help him: "I rummaged through my father's library, reading whatever I could on God, the trinity, spirit, consciousness. I devoured the books, but came away none the wiser. I always found myself thinking, 'They don't know either.' I even searched about in my father's Luther Bible."[2]

Further, the teachings of Christian faith contradicted his theories of psychological wholeness. Experiencing the shadow aspects alongside the good qualities forms the basis of individuation, that is, becoming a whole person. Since Christian doctrine presents God as perfect goodness and moral perfection as life's goal, the shadow side of life is absent from the whole person. Therefore, faith in Christian doctrines excludes parts of the whole person, namely, the negative sides or the shadowy unknown. It stops one from accepting all of one's experiences and arrests psychological growth.

For this reason Jung's religion brought him to the point of saying: "Since I knew from experience that God was not offended by any blasphemy, that on the contrary He could even encourage it, because He wished to evoke not only man's bright and positive side but also his darkness and ungodliness...."[3] Jung's God will encourage blasphemy, darkness, and ungodliness—flat contradictions of 1 John 1:5 ("God is light and in him is no darkness"), Colossians 1:12-13 ("We give thanks to the Father who has made you fit for a share in the lot of the saints in light, who delivered us from the authority of darkness and transferred us into the kingdom of the Son of his love"), and other New Testament texts.

Second, Jung emphasized personal experience of God had to replace faith in dogma. Once in a British Broadcasting Company (BBC) interview, when asked if he believed in God, he replied, "I do not believe, I know." This was in stark contrast to his father, a minister of the Reformed church in Switzerland, whose struggle with religious doubts caused him great grief. Jung lost respect for his father and his religion because of the fear of experience:

> That was what my father had not understood, I thought; he had failed to experience the will of God, had opposed it for the best of reasons and out of the deepest faith.... But he did not know the immediate living God who stands, omnipotent and free, above His Bible and His church, who calls upon man to partake of his freedom, and can force him to renounce his own views and convictions in order to fulfill without reserve the command of God. In his trial of human courage God refuses to abide by human traditions, no matter how sacred. In His omnipotence He will see to it that nothing really evil comes of such tests of courage.[4]

Jung had broken free of the fear of direct experience, after finally giving in to visualizing a fantasy of God on his golden throne in heaven dropping an enormous turd to shatter a cathedral roof.[5] Not only did he learn to accept his experience, but from it he concluded that God himself had a shadow side, denied by Christian doctrine. This and other unorthodox ideas "confirmed [his] conviction that in religious matters only experience counted."[6]

Because of Christianity's suppression of experience and doubts, Jung believed that not only his father but the whole Christian tradition was one-sided and religiously neurotic. He saw a series of unhealthy results in the church. It excluded nature, repressed animals (as seen in their extinction), and neglected its own dark and inferior side— sexuality, creative fantasy, and hostility. Christianity cut itself off from primitive roots and mythology and lost its interior life. These neglected aspects caused alienation, wars, division between the sexes, and separation from the God of experience.[7] Some Catholics have examined the experiences of their dreams and fantasies and redefined God by using Jung in just this way. God becomes a whole composed of a Father/Mother or a goddess within. Christ becomes mythologized into the earth, which is being crucified through pollution and war. These and other ideas are proclaimed as true because they come from within the psyche. That does not convince me.

Third, Jung supposed that the archetypes provide the real knowledge of the world. What the church itself says about the assumption of Mary does not matter to Jung as much as his special knowledge about the real meaning of the *mandala* and other archetypes. In fact, part of the attraction of Jung's thought to Catholics is his claim to offer true insight into our religion—deeper than the official dogma. These dogmas are the products of the conscious life and do not grasp the unconscious meaning that knowledge of the archetypes provides. For example, I recall some preachers in the Catholic charismatic renewal who redefined holiness as wholeness. One insisted on his need to forsake his vow of celibacy in order to find the wholeness of the male and female principles through marriage.

Gnosticism and Jung. This kind of thinking resembles some aspects of gnosticism, a religious movement which began in the early second century. The gnostics believed that the material world was evil, created by an evil deity or by emanations of the deities. Only the inner, spiritual world was good. The way out of the evil material world into the good spiritual world was through *gnosis*, the Greek word for knowledge. A variety of leaders from many different sects offered secret knowledge to their followers as a way of interpreting Christ's real meaning.

Jung was not gnostic to the extent that he did not consider the physical world to be evil. In fact, he believed that parallels between psychology and physics suggests "a possible ultimate *one-ness* of both fields of reality that physics and psychology study—that is, a psychophysical one-ness of all life phenomena."[8] On this issue Jung is not gnostic. Yet note how New Agers can use this statement as a psychologist's support for monism, the belief that everything in the world is ultimately one, not distinct.

Jung *is* gnostic, though, to the extent that he believed his knowledge of the psyche, especially his hypothesis of the collective unconscious and its archetypes, unlocked the real meaning of religion and personality. In spite of the church's explanations of its doctrine, Jung could give the real meaning based on his understanding of the archetypes. This comes close to faith in *gnosis* or secret knowledge.

Does Jung really take a gnostic approach to psychology, or is this merely my personal interpretation? Let us look at Jung's own words in the texts of his writings.

In 1909, after a seven-week trip to America with Freud, Jung read through "a mountain of mythological material, then through the Gnostic writers, and ended in total confusion.... It was as if I were in an imaginary madhouse and were beginning to treat and analyze all the centaurs, nymphs, gods, and goddesses... as though they were my patients.[9]

At this stage of his development, he claims to take a scientist's approach. Nine years later, in 1918, he returned to the study of gnosticism and its later, medieval form, alchemy:

> Between 1918 and 1926 I had seriously studied the Gnostic writers, for they too had been confronted with the primal world of the unconscious and had dealt with its contents, with images that were obviously contaminated with the world of instinct. Just how they understood these images remains difficult to say, in view of the paucity of the accounts—which, moreover, mostly stem from their opponents, the Church Fathers. It seems to me highly unlikely that they had a psychological conception of them. But the gnostics were too remote for me to establish any link with them in regard to the questions that were confronting me.... But when I began to understand alchemy I realized that it represented the historical link with Gnosticism, and that a continuity therefore existed between past and present. Grounded in the natural philosophy of the Middle Ages, alchemy formed the bridge on the one hand into the past, to Gnosticism, and on the other into the future, to the modern psychology of the unconscious.[10]

Not only did Jung take academic interest in gnosticism and its medieval child, alchemy, but he used it as a key to understanding modern psychology.

Few ancient gnostic texts were known when Jung began his research. A cache of them were discovered at Nag Hammadi, Egypt, after World War II. Nonetheless, Jung remained content with searching the alchemical texts for gnostic ideas to develop his view of psychology. In fact, he writes: "Through Paracelsus I was finally led to discuss the nature of alchemy in relation to religion and psychology—or, to put it another way, of alchemy as a form of religious philosophy. This I did in *Psychology and Alchemy* (1944)."[11]

Paracelsus was a Swiss physician and alchemist of the

Renaissance (1493-1541). He taught that we can know nature only because we are part of nature. Therefore, we can know God only because we are God.[12] Again, gnostic ideas, this time from the pantheist Paracelsus, became a basis of Jung's view of religion and psychology. He even accepted a form of pantheism when he says, "Like every other being, I am a splinter of the infinite deity, but I cannot contrast myself with any animal, any plant or any stone."[13] Still closer in thought to Paracelsus, Jung writes, "God has a personality and is the ego of the universe, just as I myself am the ego of my psychic and physical being."[14] Jung's gnostic ideas brought him not only to monism but to pantheism, making him a great source for what would become New Age thought.

The gnostic thought of the alchemists also influenced Jung's ideas of Christ as a "psychological figure," parallel to the philosopher's stone with which the alchemists sought to transform all matter. "My own attempt in comparing analytical psychology and Christianity led to the question of Christ as a psychological figure. As early as 1944, in *Psychology and Alchemy*, I had been able to demonstrate the parallelism between the Christ figure and the central concept of the alchemists, the *lapis*, or stone."[15]

This is no longer the Jesus Christ of the Bible or church teaching. The differences between Jung's doctrine and authentic Christian faith are immense. Gnostic ideas and dependence on his own inner experiences led Jung to treat the Christian doctrines as psychological symbols. This separates his philosophy from saving faith, as anyone who reads him today should note.

Fr. Robert Sears, S.J., insightfully writes that Jung saw faith as "an unquestioning submission that would hinder individuation,"[16] thereby resulting in the loss of freedom and independence. For Jung, the process of individuation is the key to life, so everything, including Christian doctrine, must submit to the test of how it aids the individuation process. What

Jung misses, according to Sears, is the need to relate to Jesus. Jesus "reconciles all things in himself, making peace through the blood of his cross, whether things on earth or things in heaven" (Col 1:20). Therefore, "Jesus is the key to the reconciling love so needed in our world."[17]

Jung has more than missed the point about needing to personally relate to the Lord Jesus Christ, he explicitly rejects it! He reflected on his first reception of communion in his father's Reformed church as follows: "I had observed no sign of 'communion,' of 'union, becoming one with...' With whom? With Jesus? Yet he was only a man who had died 1860 years ago. Why should a person become one with him? He was called the 'Son of God'—a demigod, therefore, like the Greek heroes: how then could an ordinary person become one with him? This was called the 'Christian religion,' but none of it had anything to do with God as I had experienced Him."[18]

The Christian faith professes that Jesus is no mere demigod or Greek hero. He is truly God the Son, the Word of God "who was in the beginning and who was God, through whom all things were made and without whom nothing was made" (Jn 1:1,3). Christ calls himself the true vine, and we are the branches united to him. Unless we are united to him like branches on the vine, we cannot do anything (Jn 15:1-6). Union with Christ is not merely possible, it is absolutely necessary. Teilhard said, "Unity differentiates," which means that true union with Christ does not destroy our individuality or personality. Rather, the more closely we are united to Christ, the more clearly distinguished becomes the unique gift God has made each of us to be.

St. Paul emphasizes the same teaching about union with Christ (1 Cor 12), when he teaches that by our baptism we are members of the body of Christ, his church. The Holy Spirit makes us into members of this body, each with a unique role and place within the church. It is precisely our union with God through Jesus and in the Holy Spirit that enables us to become individuated. God's relationship with us effects this transformation by his freely given grace.

OTHER PROBLEMS WITH JUNG'S DOCTRINES

My love for Jung and my commitment to Christianity put me into a quandary: Jung reinterpreted Christianity along mythical and gnostic lines. I began to see the ramifications of his approach in further teachings about God, Christ, Christ's mission, the Holy Spirit, and the church—all of which contradicted Catholic teaching. Let me present Jung's ideas on these topics one by one.

Jungian Concept of God. We have already pointed out how Jung tended to believe in monism and pantheism: everything is one; and that oneness is God, so everything is God. This is most clearly seen in the quote, "Like every other being, I am a splinter of the infinite deity, but I cannot contrast myself with any animal, any plant or any stone."[19] He develops further ideas of monism and the inability to distinguish humans and non-humans: "For nature seemed, like myself, to have been set aside by God as non-divine, although created by Him as an expression of Himself. Nothing could persuade me that 'in the image of God' applied only to man. In fact it seemed to me that the high mountains, the rivers, lakes, trees, flowers, and animals far better exemplified the essence of God than men with their ridiculous clothes, their meanness, vanity, mendacity, and abhorrent egotism."[20] One of my difficulties with this passage comes from Jung not distinguishing the essence of human beings from non-human entities, despite his emphasis on human individuation in therapy.

Furthermore, Jung ignores the biblical texts on the beauty and wonder of creation: Genesis 1-2; Psalms 8, 24, 95-99, 104, 148-149, along with Proverbs 8 and many passages in Sirach, Wisdom, and the prophets. Creation does proclaim the glory of God (Ps 19:1-6), without being God. To be sure, humans behave sinfully and tarnish the fact that they are images of God, while the rest of creation does not sin. Yet is not that fact true precisely because humans, like God, have free will and intellect, setting them above the other creatures but at the same time making it possible for them to rebel against God?

Adam was able to name the animals in Genesis 2:19, but they could not name him. Certainly this dominion is no warrant for destroying other species or abusing nature. That behavior is sinful, as classic Catholic moral theology teaches. Certainly some people abuse nature, but that is no reason for Jung to deny the superiority of humans over the animals. After all, Jung can make this moral judgment. Animals, plants, mountains, and lakes cannot.

I had another problem with Jung's doctrine of God when he claimed that God wants people to sin.

> That was clear, too, from the serpent, whom God had created before them, obviously so that it could induce Adam and Eve to sin. God in his omniscience had arranged everything so that the first parents would have to sin. *Therefore it was God's intention that they should sin.*[21]

> God had also created Adam and Eve in such a way that they had to think what they did not at all want to think. He had done that in order to find out whether they were obedient.[22]

> God could at most have felt "satisfaction" with paradise, but then He Himself had taken good care that the glory of paradise should not last too long by planting in it that poisonous serpent, the devil. Had He taken satisfaction in that too?[23]

These three quotes show that Jung blamed God for the Fall of Adam and Eve. At times I held God responsible for my sins, telling myself that God would permit me to do things he forbade people in general. Such was a small child's concept of an indulgent Grandfather God.

Jung blames God for Adam and Eve's sin, instead of recognizing their free will to choose to disobey the one commandment God had given them. This is exactly the same tactic Adam took: "The woman whom *you* put here gave me to eat." It was God's fault for creating the woman. Then Eve went on to blame the serpent (Gn 3:12-13). This shows that there really is nothing new under the sun. The same old temptations continue to trip us up, like shifting blame away from those who actually commit the sins.

Not only does Jung blame God for our first parents' sin, but for his own sin as well. "You don't know that God wants to force me to do wrong, that He forces me to think abominations in order to experience his grace."[24] This idea could become quite convenient for some people, like a couple who, though they admitted to living an adulterous relationship, professed that they were saved, so God must have wanted them to commit adultery. Jung's ideas lend support to those who prefer to justify their sins rather than confess them to God and ask for his mercy. Such people can feel justified in blaming God for their wrongdoing as well as the havoc that their sins cause them and others.

For Jung, God causes these sins because God himself contains both goodness and evil. "I also found it extremely unsatisfying that the philosophers offered no opinions or explanations about the dark deeds of God... for the light and darkness of God seemed to me facts that could be understood even though they oppressed my feelings."[25] Since God is both good and bad, dark and light, he expects the same from human beings. "... I knew from experience that God was not offended by any blasphemy, that on the contrary He could even encourage it because He wished to evoke not only man's bright and positive side but also his darkness and ungodliness."[26]

Naturally, Jung opposed Christian teaching. His own ideas fly in the face of Scripture and church doctrine, like 1 John 1:5. My own experience of God and his moral demands in Scripture has been a call to be always better than I tend to be. Sin comes from me easily enough, and condoning my own wrongdoing never brings me real peace. I did not believe my own lame excuses, how can I really expect God to? Rather, I find peace when I examine my actions in the light of God's call to be holy, compassionate, and perfect as he is (see Lv 19:2; Lk 6:36; Mt 5:48), making my goals concrete. When I disobey or fall short, I need to recognize my sin and take responsibility for it. Then I can ask God to transform me by his love, since that is his nature (1 Jn 4:16, "God is love"). By bringing the darkness of my sins to God's light and letting Jesus, the "light of the world" (Jn 8:12), shine on that darkness, I find true peace. In light of my Christian experience of God, Jung's view was not only untrue to scriptural teaching but personally unsatisfying.

Jungian Concept of Jesus. Though a minister's son, Jung took a negative view of Jesus Christ when he was still a boy:

> I began to distrust Lord Jesus. He lost the aspect of a big, comforting, benevolent bird and became associated with the gloomy black men in frock coats, top hats, and shiny black boots who busied themselves with the black box [coffin].[27]

> While it became increasingly impossible for me to adopt a positive attitude to Lord Jesus, I remember that from the time I was eleven the idea of God began to interest me.... God was not complicated by my distrust. Moreover, he was not a person in a black robe, and not Lord Jesus of the pictures, draped with brightly colored clothes, with whom people behaved so familiarly.[28]

Lord Jesus was to me unquestionably a man and therefore a fallible figure, or else a mere mouthpiece of the Holy Ghost.[29]

My own experience of Christ was so different from Jung's because Christ became increasingly personal and real. As novices we made a thirty-day retreat using the Spiritual Exercises of St. Ignatius Loyola. My meditations on the Gospels, along with prayerful conversation with Jesus, changed my life for the better. I let Jesus get to know me, even in my sinful weakness. On the retreat I came to trust that he loves me as I am, yet loves me enough to make me better than I am. Jung's experience of Jesus seemed quite foreign to mine.

Jung also interpreted Christ as a psychological figure who represented the self. As he wrote, "My attempt to bring analytical psychology into relation with Christianity ultimately led to the question of Christ as a psychological figure."[30] Since Jung was primarily concerned with the way Christ affected the psyche of his patients, Christ became a symbol rather than a Savior, just like the alchemists' "philosopher's stone." This stone, if found, could change base metals into gold, like Christ could transform personalities. To Jung, both are equal symbols of transformation, but for me an impersonal stone could never take the place of the personal Jesus Christ. As God, Christ can transcend time and place and become present to me anywhere and at any time, whether at Mass or private prayer. The "philosopher's stone" was a myth I could make up anywhere, but it would nonetheless be my own creation, not my redeeming Creator.

Jung also stated that Christ is, like Buddha, a symbol of the self, with different strengths and weaknesses:

Christ—like Buddha—is an embodiment of the self, but in an altogether different sense. Both stood for an overcoming of the world: Buddha out of rational insight; Christ as a foredoomed sacrifice. In Christianity more is suffered, in Buddhism more is seen and done. Both paths are right, but in the Indian sense Buddha is the more complete human being. He is a historical personality, and therefore easier for men to understand. Christ is at once a historical man and God, and therefore much more difficult to comprehend. At bottom he was not comprehensible even to himself; he knew only that he had to sacrifice himself, that this course was imposed upon him from within. His sacrifice happened to him like an act of destiny. Buddha lived out his life and died at an advanced age, whereas Christ's activity as Christ probably lasted no more than a year.[31]

Here Jung says that both paths are right, which conflicts with our Lord's claim in John 14:6, "I am the way, the truth and the life; no one comes to the Father except through me." While Buddha teaches a path to *nirvana* (the state of annihilation of the self), Christ is the path to the Father. Instead of annihilation, Christ promises us eternal life at home in heaven with a Father who loves us infinitely. Setting self-annihilation as the goal of my existence could not compare with the eternal and infinite love the Father has in store for me.

A second problem in this passage is that Christ's claim to be God makes him less complete than Buddha, who is only human. The apparent logic of Jung's reasoning here is that people can understand the merely human Buddha better, therefore, he is more complete. Jesus could not even comprehend himself, according to Jung, therefore he is less complete than the simpler-to-comprehend Buddha. Keep in mind that Jung, like most New Agers today, admitted to looking at Christ "in the Indian sense." This means a mythical view of the way Christ affects us. It allows Jung, like New

Agers, to pick and choose the parts of Christ that fit into his system of thought and consciousness. Anything that does not fit can be neglected.

Jung has this comment on the historical person of Jesus Christ:

> As I delved into all these matters the question of the historical person, of Jesus the man, also came up. It is of importance because the collective mentality of his time— one might also say: the archetype which was already constellated, the primordial image of the Anthropos—was condensed in him, an almost unknown Jewish prophet. The ancient idea of the Anthropos, whose roots lie in Jewish tradition on the one hand and in the Egyptian Horus myth on the other, had taken possession of the people at the beginning of the Christian era, for it was part of the Zeitgeist. It was essentially concerned with the Son of Man, God's own son, who stood opposed to the deified Augustus, the ruler of the world. This idea fastened upon the originally Jewish problem of the Messiah and made it a world problem.[32]

Here again Jung takes a mythic approach to Christ, though this time from the perspective of Egyptian mythology. Remember that much of the gnostic tradition has its roots in Egypt and tries to unite Egyptian mythology, Greek thought, and Christian symbols into a new religious system. This is exactly what Jung and New Agers do. For Jung, the significance of the historical Jesus comes from the fact that he symbolized the main archetype of his times. He combined the Jewish Messiah, the Egyptian Horus myth, and the God-man (*Anthropos* is Greek for man) representing all humanity.

In another text, Jung again interprets Jesus Christ, according to the lines of Egyptian mythology, here in the Osiris myth.

The myth of Osiris from Egypt was followed by the Christ myth, despite the theologians' claim that the New Testament has little to do with Egyptology. Jung connects Christ's genealogy of three groups of fourteen names with the Egyptian Heb-Sed festival. Egyptians "celebrated every thirty years to reaffirm Pharaoh as God's son" with a procession of fourteen of his ancestors. Christ is God's son and had to be more exalted than Pharaoh, so three times fourteen generations had to be written to conform to the thrice holy formula from Isaiah 6. The statements about Christ that have been handed down historically are "mythological statements intimately connected with the myth of Osiris. That is why Christianity spread into Egypt without meeting the slightest resistance."[33]

The considered opinion of New Testament scholars does not matter to Jung. If he believes that Egyptian mythology has influenced the story of Jesus Christ, then it is so. The lack of evidence does not matter; only Jung's opinion counts. Because there are three groups of fourteen names each in Christ's genealogy, the significance is based on the Egyptian Heb-Sed festival. Even though the numerical value of the letters of David's name adds up to fourteen, which is the ancient interpretation of Jesus' genealogies, Jung is right.

Furthermore, the god Osiris represented the dead Pharaoh who came back to life and ruled over the world of the dead. Some humans, especially nobles, and sacred animals became identified with Osiris to find life in the world of the dead. In some texts, Osiris was the judge of the dead upon their entrance to the underworld. Jung insists that Osiris is therefore the proper way to understand Christ. Therefore, Christianity spread into Egypt so easily because of this similarity to the Osiris myth!

Commonly New Agers, like Edgar Cayce, Ruth Montgomery, and others who believe in reincarnation, claim that in past lives they were pharaohs or Egyptian priests and priestesses. They are frequently attracted to myths about Egyptian life and religion simply because it is so fascinating. Jung's Egyptian mythological interpretation brings Christ within the Egyptian orbit and makes him acceptable to the New Age mental framework.

Jung fails to explain that Jesus Christ, unlike Edgar Cayce, never claimed to have been a pharaoh who died and became the king of the underworld. Rather, Scripture says that after Christ died on the cross, he descended to preach to the spirits in "prison," that is the souls of everyone who died "in the days of Noah" (1 Pt 3:18-20). However, Christ did not remain in the realm of the dead as their king. On the third day after his death, he rose from the dead and came to life in a glorified body. He was physically raised and glorified, touched by disciples, and seen by nearly five hundred and twenty-five witnesses (1 Cor 15:4-8). The story of Christ's resurrection is nothing at all like the myth of Osiris, making the Egyptian myth the wrong way to view Christ.

Jung and Christ's Mission. Jung's interpretation of Christ's mission to the world includes both ambiguity about Christ's identity and false teaching about God's relationship to evil. "Christ is the suffering servant of God, and so was Job. In the case of Christ the sins of the world are the cause of suffering, and the suffering of the Christian is the general answer. This leads inescapably to the question: Who is responsible for these sins? In the final analysis it is God who created the world and its sins, and who therefore became Christ in order to suffer the fate of humanity."[34] On one hand Jung accepts the biblical doctrine of Christ as the Suffering Servant who died so that our sins can be forgiven. In the last lines, Jung intimates that God became Christ in order to suffer the human fate of suffering. This contrasts with another statement by Jung: "Lord Jesus was to me unquestionably a man and therefore a fallible figure, or else a mere mouthpiece of the Holy Ghost."[35] These statements confuse the reader about the crucial question of life, posed by Jesus our Lord: "Who do you say I am?" (Mt 16:15). Jung's waffling on the identity of Jesus leaves his works open to New Age interpretations of Jesus, not genuine Christian teaching.

New Agers teach that Christ is a state of consciousness that each human can receive or attain. In this sense, everyone can "become" Christ and therefore become divine. Once in a course on St. Paul, I asked my Jesuit professor whether we could call ourselves "christs" since we used the name "Christian." Influenced by Jung's statement that God "became Christ," I wondered whether we could become christs too. The professor, taken aback by such an odd question, resoundingly said, "No, of course not."

The answer I needed came from studying the authentic Christian, biblical teaching that Jesus Christ is both God and human. St. John teaches that Jesus is the Word of God who was with God and who is God (Jn 1:1-4). This Word is fully divine and truly became flesh (Jn 1:14) in the womb of Mary. From the moment of his conception, he is fully God and fully human.

Humans, on the other hand, cannot become God. We remain humans forever, though we will live forever. Those humans redeemed by Christ Jesus become adopted children of God (Rom 8:15). They will live forever in the resurrection of the dead.

The following is one way I approach New Agers who teach that humans become Christ. I ask them to be open and honest—open to the gospel and honest in accepting the words that Jesus says about himself. Then I invite them to read the Scripture. That is better than reading the text to them. That way the Holy Spirit works in their minds with the Word of God which he inspired. Also while they are reading the text, they cannot think about counterarguments but have to listen to it more carefully.

Ask the New Ager to explain what the passage means in its context, using the actual words of the text instead of what they once thought the passage might have meant. My friend, the late Walter Martin, used to call this having them "fall on the sword" of Scripture. Even when the New Ager walks away without understanding your reasons, God's holy Word continues to stir within his or her heart.

Jung's teaching on Christ is connected to his belief that God is the source of sin, having created sin along with the rest of the world. "Jung... went on to mention the symbolism attached to Christ, indicating opposites in his nature, as, for instance, the Leviathan, the Lion, the Serpent, the Black Raven, and his crucifixion between two thieves. Then the symbolism became astrological. Jung stated, "At the birth of Christ, Saturn the maleficent god and Jupiter the beneficent god were so near to each other that they were almost one star, that is, the star of Bethlehem, when the new self, Christ, good and evil, was born."[36] Not only did Jung teach that God created evil, but the new self, Christ, somehow personifies good and evil. He continues his ideas that Christ is a symbol and the new self. Of course, this agrees with Jung's ideas about God as the source of good and evil, having a shadow side.

Jung again interprets Christ from the perspective of mythology, the mythology of astrology, and the personifications of the planets Saturn and Jupiter. The conjunction of two planets—Saturn representing the dark side and Jupiter the good side—becomes Jung's mythological and astrological interpretation of the star of Bethlehem that appeared to the magi when Christ was born. Jung frequently interprets Christ astrologically, which we will address in the next chapter. Here it becomes the basis for Jung calling Christ the "new self" and "good and evil." Jung's astrological interpretation of Jesus' birth being dominated by the conjunction of evil and good planets means that Jesus is both evil and good.

I could not reconcile these teachings with the scriptural doctrine that Jesus was completely without sin. The Gospels portray Jesus Christ as good. Other passages simply state that

Jesus is free of all sin, deceit, and evil. One clear text is Hebrews 4:15, which says that Jesus Christ is "not a high priest unable to sympathize with our weaknesses, but he has been tempted in all ways like us, except for sin." Temptation comes to him from various sources: Satan in the desert, the crowds who wished to make him king (Jn 6:15), St. Peter who tried to stop him from talking about his coming death (Mt 16:22; Mk 8:32), and the taunting crowds at the cross (Mt 27:39-44). Nonetheless, Jesus never sins by yielding to any temptation. First John 3:5 says: "You know that the reason he was manifested was that he might bear sins, and sin is not in him." First Peter 2:22 claims: "He did not sin, nor was guile found in his mouth." These passages reflect the prophecy in Isaiah 53:9: "A grave was given to him among the wicked, and his tomb among the rich, though he had done no violence and there was no deceit in his mouth."

Jung's Jesus Christ did not add up to the gospel portrayal at all. I had to decide between Scripture and Jung regarding my understanding and relationship with Christ. I chose Scripture, as the church has always done, without the slightest regret.

Jung and the Holy Spirit. Jung's distortion of good and evil in God does not end with Christ but includes the Holy Spirit. "For me the Holy Ghost was a manifestation of the inconceivable God. The workings of the Holy Ghost were not only sublime but also partook of that strange and even questionable quality which characterized the deeds of Yahweh, whom I naively identified with the Christian image of God."[37]

I noticed that Jung separated Yahweh, the Hebrew name of God in the Old Testament, from the "Christian image of God." My studies of early church history showed that this was the same error made by Marcion, the son of a bishop, who claimed that the God of the Old Testament was evil, while the Father revealed by Jesus was a good God. This led

Marcion and his followers to reject the Old Testament as Scripture and to exclude the New Testament books written by Jews, except for some parts of St. Paul. This left Marcion with St. Luke's Gospel. Jung's division between Yahweh and the Christian God would end up with the same problem.

Again, Jung finds that the Holy Spirit shares in the "strange and even questionable" qualities of God. God, Jesus, and the Holy Spirit contain morally dark sides which reflect the dark side of each human being. I have experienced those qualities neither in Scripture nor in my devotional life, though God has challenged me morally and spiritually. I cannot give my mind and heart to Jung's theology.

Jung's View of the Church. Jung had a very negative view of the Reformed church where he grew up and where his father was pastor.

> Church gradually became a place of torment to me. For there men dared to preach aloud—I am tempted to say, shamelessly—about God, about His intentions and actions.... Moreover, I was certain that this was the wrong way to reach God, for I knew, knew from experience, that this grace was accorded only to one who fulfilled the will of God without reservation.... To me it seemed that one's duty was to explore daily the will of God.... It seemed often to me that religious precepts were being put in place of the will of God.[38]

Like Jung, I wanted to do the will of God. Seeking God's will and desiring to act on it was the goal of the Spiritual Exercises of St. Ignatius, the basis of Jesuit spirituality. Therefore, Jung's claim that "grace was accorded only to one who fulfilled the will of God" sounded attractive. However, closer examination revealed some errors. First, grace does not only come as a reward for doing God's will. Grace is also what makes it *possible* to do God's will at all. Second, the statement omits the fact that Christ came to establish a church, with Peter as the rock upon which it is founded for all time (Mt 16:18). The church is the body of Christ here on earth. We are called to belong to it as the only way to be united to Christ, as members of that body, in intimate union with him (1 Cor 12; Jn 15:1-7).

Jung wrote further about religion: "... I understood religion as something that God did to me; it was an act on His part, to which I must simply yield, for he was the stronger. My 'religion' recognized no human relationship to God, for how could anyone relate to something so little known as God?"[39] Human relationship to God was impossible to Jung's mind. Religion meant obeying God with no possibility of knowing him! "The arch sin of faith, it seemed to me, was that it forestalled experience."[40] The key was an experience of God—not the experience of a personal relationship but of an impersonal God. Jung's ideas appeared self-contradictory to me—requiring personal experience of an impersonal and unknowable God. Further, they contradicted my own experience in the church. The saints claimed to have had personal experiences with God, and they showed other people ways to know God. Trusting their experience—particularly that of St. Ignatius—proved more reliable than Jung's doctrines.

Jung personally rejected Christianity as his religion. Though he believed that people today live "in the Christian myth," his own "honest" answer was, "For me, it is not what I live by."[41] His father's faith and practice also kept him back.

> ... I saw how hopelessly [my father] was entrapped by the church and its theological thinking. They had blocked all avenues by which he might have reached God directly, and then faithlessly abandoned him. Now I understood the deepest meaning of my earlier experience: God Himself had disavowed theology and the church founded upon it. On the other hand God condoned this theology,

as He condoned so much else. It seemed ridiculous to me to suppose that men were responsible for such developments.... I was equally sure that none of the theologians had ever seen "the light that shineth in the darkness" with his own eyes, for if they had they would not have been able to teach a "theological religion," which seemed quite inadequate to me, since there was nothing to do with it but believe it without hope.[42]

In fact, he felt that it was God's will that he leave the church. "For God's sake I now found myself cut off from the church and from my father's and everybody else's faith."[43]

WHY FOCUS ON JUNG'S DOCTRINE?

Many of Jung's psychological insights helped me discover insights into myself. His notion of the shadow—the dark, unknown side of each person—gave me courage to admit and accept problems that frightened me. My "individuation" or maturing process was helped by honest acceptance of my negative qualities. His description of archetypes suggested some ways to get a handle on images in my dreams.

My problems with Jung do not necessarily stem from the psychological insights he offers. In the hands of a professional, these can be useful for personal growth. However, I do have problems when Catholics use Jung's gnostic and mythic interpretations of God, Christ, the Holy Spirit, the church, doctrine, and morals. On one hand, recognizing our own shadow may prepare us for deep personal and spiritual growth. Perhaps a conversion based on deep repentance may result from recognition of the shadow. However, projecting our shadow onto God the Father, Christ, and the Holy Spirit forces us to contradict Scripture and the roots of our faith, as the discussion throughout this chapter indicates. Interpreting Catholic faith through the lens of Egyptian,

Oriental, or Greek myths distorts the revelation given through Jesus Christ. Insisting on private experience in a gnostic or alchemical way makes humans the norm for religion rather than letting God set the norms for us. I cannot accept this.

Jung's fascination with the occult sprang up frequently in the quotations from his books, especially from his autobiography. The occult and spiritism constitute a prominent theme in his life and work. This was enough to influence me to take up a number of occult practices while I was a seminarian, such as the *I Ching* and astrology. In my hunger to know more about myself, I became willing to use any tool that would help me see my unknown or shadow side. The next chapters will share some ways I pursued Jungian concepts in my practice of astrology and the enneagram.

THREE

Astrology: Grounding the Stars in a Sense of Science

JUNG'S INTEREST IN THE OCCULT impressed me from my first reading of *Man and His Symbols*. At first, I was bothered by the Baltimore Catechism's prohibition against any practice of the occult. However, Jung's scientific approach put these worries to rest. I only wanted to study astrology and the *I Ching* to help others (and myself) gain deeper self-knowledge and psychological health.

When I returned to classes in Detroit that fall, my Bahai friends and teachers from the Buckminster Fuller course taught me a scientific and psychological technique of casting horoscopes. They showed me how to use *ephemerides,* the books which record the astrological location of each planet. I devoured as many books on astrology as my budget could afford to supplement what my friends taught me.

For more background, I registered in an astronomy course for non-physics majors like me. The professor, Dr. Blass, then president of a Detroit astronomical society, was a fine teacher. He believed in astrology but had no theory to explain its operation. He was certain that gravity and light had nothing to do with its effectiveness, yet somehow it really worked.

He lived in Germany through the war and told me a scary story about its influence on Hitler and the outcome of D-Day. Hitler's belief in astrology, spiritism, and the occult not only supported his racist theories[1] but helped determine his policies. According to Dr. Blass, when the Allies learned about Hitler's faith in astrology, they asked astrologers to tell them what Hitler's astrologers might be saying. While the Allies sent information through the spy network *confirming* Hitler's occult information, they did the opposite. The landing at Normandy in June was astrologically bad. A later landing at Pas de Calais would have been more logical and astrologically more propitious too. Spies passed on the Pas de Calais landing site and Hitler kept Panzer divisions there for three days after the Allies had landed at Normandy with their main force. This story was disconcerting, though, because it showed how astrology led to Hitler's undoing. Obviously, it could be a dangerous tool. I should have paid attention to this danger, but I didn't.

Merrily I cast horoscopes for friends, Jesuit and lay. Having greater knowledge about other persons than they have about themselves is an emotional rush. When others came to me to learn about themselves, it fueled my pride. As a teacher at St. Xavier High, I even taught a mini-course in astrology. It was a lot of fun and I did not want to stop.

The only negative feedback to casting the charts came from a long-haired Jesus freak at the University of Detroit. He attended some of our weekly prayer sessions and expressed real concern about the morality of casting horoscopes in light of the Bible's prohibition of astrology. I dismissed his words easily by insisting on the scientific nature of astrology. Jung used it in therapy and Dr. Blass believed in it, so it must be scientific and therefore okay. Eventually, I learned that astrology has absolutely *no* scientific basis and even less theological grounding.

I will explore here how Jung viewed astrology and then

explain how astrology works to demonstrate its scientific, psychological, and biblical folly.

JUNG'S FASCINATION WITH ASTROLOGY

Astrology has had its ups and downs throughout its four-thousand-year history. Today with the rise of the New Age Movement, it has increased in popularity. In America at least one-third of the population firmly believes in astrology and as many as 90 percent are open to it. About ten thousand professional and four hundred and fifty thousand amateur astrologers work in the United States, and nearly two thousand five hundred newspapers carry horoscopes as a regular feature. Its popularity has grown in Europe as well.[2] In Asia it never lost popularity.

The fascination with the occult reaches far back in Jung's family. His maternal grandfather held weekly séances to carry on conversations with his first wife. His mother, Emily Jung, had an interest in anything Oriental and in the preternatural (beyond normal, explicable experiences). Young Carl had heard many stories about spirits from the Swiss country folk too. Apparently all this predisposed Carl to the occult.

Jung first studied spiritism as a university student. He read a history of spiritism and connected it with the stories he heard as a boy.

> I could not help seeing that the phenomena described in the book were in principle much the same as the stories I had heard again and again in the country since my earliest childhood. The material without a doubt was authentic.... Rather it must be connected with the objective behavior of the human psyche. The observations of the spiritualists, weird and questionable as they seemed to

me, were the first accounts I had seen of objective psychic phenomena.... I read virtually the whole of the literature available to me at the time.... I, too, was not certain of the absolute reliability of the reports, but why, after all, should there not be ghosts? How did we know that something was "impossible"? For myself I found such possibilities extremely interesting and attractive. They added another dimension to my life; the world gained depth and background. Could, for example, dreams have anything to do with ghosts?[3]

His best friend during his student days was Albert Oeri. Oeri also says that Jung was preoccupied with the occult in early student days and led a group of students in this interest.

... [He] had courageously schooled himself, intensively studying occult literature, conducting parapsychological experiments, and finally standing by the convictions he derived therefrom, except where corrected by the result of more careful and detailed psychological studies. He was appalled that the official scientific position of the day toward occult phenomena was simply to deny their existence, rather than to investigate and explain them. For this reason, spiritualists like Zollner and Crookes, about whose teachings he could speak for hours, became for him heroic martyrs of science. Among his friends and relatives he found participants for séances.[4]

Jung was not content to lecture his fellow students. His pet dachshund also had to endure lectures because the dog had psychic powers. "Already a dog lover, he would earnestly lecture a young dachshund he had acquired, claiming that the animal not only understood every word but also had parapsychological potential which caused it to whimper whenever occultic presences were active."[5]

Oeri said that Jung was afraid to walk home from their student pub, the Brio, late at night because the "Nightingale Woods" between the pub and home were haunted. The tree where a certain Dr. Goetz was murdered was a particular cause of anxiety for Jung. After induction into the Swiss army, he took to carrying his service revolver with him, or offering it to friends, when walking through those woods.[6]

As one biographer wrote, "Thus to Jung spiritism was not a matter of occultism but of unknown phenomena that needed to be investigated with proper scientific methods."[7] Therefore, Jung based his doctoral dissertation on a study of spiritism. For two years he attended séances held by some relatives with a fifteen-year-old cousin, Helene Preiswerk, on his mother's side. He found the movements of the table questionable, but he accepted other coincidences without suspicion of fraud. Later the evidence of the girl's romantic crush on Jung and her fraudulent practices while in the trances became public knowledge. Nonetheless, Jung used the "content of the communications" from the spirits as material for his doctoral thesis. He produced a "deeply thought-out academic thesis which gave a profound analysis of the interlocking relationship between psychic and spiritualistic phenomena."[8]

Jung's marriage of the occult and science fit the attitude of the day. Many nineteenth-century scientists were taken in by spiritists, including Nobel Prize winners.[9] Perhaps those who scurried to the study of the occult wanted to discount their own Christian or Jewish background. Humans are made to be spiritual. St. Augustine wrote in his *Confessions,* "Our hearts are restless until they rest in You." When people reject the spiritual life offered by God, they opt for a bogus spirituality. In part, this criticism applies to Jung.

Brome's biography of Jung presents a double evaluation of Jung's scientific approach to the occult. On one hand he says, "Any skepticism about the phenomena Jung investigated has to take into account his emphasis on its psychological roots. He was not simply another recruit to the gullible ranks of spiritualism; his purpose was much more genuinely scientific."[10] However, the same biographer criticizes Jung because: "A certain lack of intellectual rigor was apparent in Jung's approach to a subject destined to become all-important, when he concluded that the repeated proliferation of stories about ghosts and psychic phenomena throughout the world was evidence for their validity."[11] These two quotes capture two sides of Jung's approach. His desire and intention was to be rigorously scientific. However, the reality is that he was less skeptical about spiritism than he was about Christianity. This was one result of his "lack of intellectual rigour."

There are two reasons to analyze Jung's spiritism. First, his pseudo-scientific approach to the occult is parallel to that which is taken by many people who get involved in the New Age Movement. Ruth Montgomery had her start as the "First Lady of the New Age Movement" by attending sessions with spiritists as an "objective" reporter. She, too, let go of her journalistic perspective when fascination with psychic phenomena overtook her. Edgar Cayce, an evangelical Sunday school teacher, gave up his belief in the Bible's condemnation of spiritism when a spirit he called "the Entity" took control of him during trances. Scientists and other "objective" persons are seduced by spiritism and the occult even in their very attempts to study them objectively.

These dangers make the biblical and church prohibitions against spiritism all the more compelling. Deuteronomy 18:9-12 is one of the clearest passages on this topic: "When you come into the land which Yahweh your God is giving to you, you shall not learn to do the abominations of those nations. There shall not be found among you one who makes his son or his daughter pass through fire, a diviner of charms, a soothsayer, a sorcerer, a magician, one who consults ghosts or familiar spirits, or who seeks the dead. Whoever does these things becomes an abomination."

The church is equally clear in warning against attendance at a séance, even out of curiosity. A Vatican decree of July 30, 1856 exhorted bishops to use every effort to suppress the abuses of the "evocation of departed spirits and other super-stitious practices of spiritism."[12] The Vatican's Holy Office was asked a series of questions: "Whether it is allowed either through a so-called medium or without one, and with or without hypnotism, to assist at any spiritualistic communica-tions or manifestations, even such as appear to be blameless or pious, either asking questions of the souls or spirits, or lis-tening to their answers, or merely looking on, even with a tacit or express protestation that one does not want to have anything to do with evil spirits?" The answer given on April 26, 1917 was no. The church is as definite as Deuteronomy in order to protect the flock of Christ from seduction by the spiritists and the spirits.

Second, Jung's scientific interest in spiritism led him to deeper involvement with it, a pattern common in many New Agers too. When I saw Jung's "scientific" involvement, I found a "scientific" basis for my own practice of the occult. There is a similar temptation for others who place their faith in Jung. As a psychologist, he lends credibility to occult behaviors.

JUNG AND THE AGE OF AQUARIUS

Gordon Young: *"Do you believe that astrology has any definite value?"*

Carl Jung: "The whole subject, of course, is controversial. But you know I once did some statistical research on astrology and my final figures were examined by mathe-maticians at the University of Chicago. They told me that they found them not without significance. Naturally, when I heard that I pricked up my ears. We are passing out of the period of the Fishes just now and into the sign of Aquarius, which may well bring some new values with it. Some people quite seriously consider that this may be of great significance in the world's imminent development."[13]

As mentioned in the Introduction, a key element in the name and definition of the New Age Movement is its belief in a coming "Age of Aquarius." According to astrological faith, a new age begins every 2,160 years, dominated by a particular astrological sign. Jung expounded on this in a number of situations. Let him explain this overview of history.

Georges Duplain: *"You speak of a change of era, of a new Platonic month, of the passage into another sign of the zodiac. What do you mean by that, what reality do such constellations have?"*

Jung: "The great astrological periods do exist. Taurus and Gemini were prehistoric periods, we don't know much about them. But Aries the Ram is closer; Alexander the Great was one of its manifestations. That was from 2000 B.C. to the beginning of the Christian era. With that era we came into the sign of the Fishes. It was not I who invented all the fish symbols there are in Christianity: the fisher of men, the *pisciculi christianorum.* Christianity has marked us deeply because it incarnates the symbols of the era so well. It goes wrong when it believes itself to be the only truth; when what it is is one of the great expressions of truth in our time. To deny it would be to throw the baby out with the bathwater. What comes next? Aquarius, the Water-pourer, the falling of water from one place to another. And the little fish [Piscis Austrinus, the Southern Fish] receiving the water from the pitcher of the Water-pourer, and whose principal star is Formalhaut, which means, 'fish's mouth.' In our era the fish is the content; with the Water-pourer, he becomes the container. It's a very strange symbol. I don't dare interpret it. So far as one can tell, it is the image of a great man approaching. One finds, besides, a lot of things about this in the Bible itself: there are more things in the Bible than the theologians can admit.

"It is a matter of experience that the symbolism changes from one sign to another, and there is the risk that this passage will be all the more difficult for the men of today and tomorrow because they no longer believe in it, no longer want to be conscious of it."[14]

Jung looks back on "three Platonic months, three aeons of conscious history." The Osiris myth was superseded by the Christ myth as that new aeon came along. This means that new versions of the same myth, not a really new myth, come along with each aeon. Hammurabi the lawgiver of Babylon felt that he was the lord of a new aeon around 2000 B.C. [though he lived in the mid-1800s], roughly the time when the Jewish tradition began. Two thousand years later came the age of Augustus Caesar, whose birth was regarded by the Romans as the birth of a savior in Virgil's *Fourth Ecologue.* Christians interpreted this as the birth of Christ.[15]

According to Jung, history is now at the end of the Piscean aeon, dominated by Christianity. That religion will fade away as the aeon of Aquarius begins, about one-hundred-fifty to two-hundred years from now. Some New Agers believe the new Age of Aquarius is already upon us.

Jung believed that the new Age of Aquarius will face both serious threats and opportunities. For instance, the atom bomb is "terribly characteristic of Aquarius, whose ruler is Uranos, the Lord of unpredictable events."[16] His solution to the threat is Jungian psychology: "A spirit of greater openness towards the unconscious, an increased attention to dreams, a sharper sense of the totality of the physical and the psychic, of their indissolubility; a livelier taste for self-knowledge. Better established mental hygiene, if you want to put it that way. The religions have tried to be this, but the result is not entirely satisfactory."[17]

Consistent with Jung's beliefs about religion (see Chapter Two) is his denial of its success. Therefore, in place of religion, people must search inside themselves. Their own unconscious, especially as experienced through dreams, will provide the self-knowledge and mental health needed for passage into the new Age of Aquarius. People have their own cure within themselves, if they will just tap their inner resources.

Instead of religion, Jung hinted that humans needed to realize that they are gods:

> Like every other being, I am a splinter of the infinite deity, but I cannot contrast myself with any animal, any plant or any stone.[18]

> As Buddha, by virtue of his insight, was far in advance of the *Brahman* gods, so Christ cried out to the Jews, "You are gods" (Jn 10:34); but men were incapable of understanding what he meant. Instead we find that the so-called Christian West, far from creating a new world, is moving with giant strides toward the possibility of destroying the world we have.[19]

The prescription to go inside one's psyche and hints of belief in the divinity of the human person play into the hands of the New Agers, who typically believe that everyone is divine. For them, the problem of human existence is that people do not have enough self-awareness to realize their divinity. Anyone who uses New Age techniques to get inside him or herself and discover complete enlightenment will realize his or her personal divinity. That is the key for entrance into the New Age. Jung again becomes a support for New Age thought.

Just as Jung looked at Christ through mythical glasses, he also saw Christ in an Aquarian perspective, much as New Agers do. The above quotes already allude to the Age of Pisces as the time of Christ. Chapter Two quotes the astrological interpretation of the star of Bethlehem as the alignment of "Saturn the maleficent god and Jupiter the beneficent god." Their alignment as the star of Bethlehem indicated to Jung that Christ, the new self, is good and evil.

Jung wrote, "It was also important to me to show how Christ could have been astrologically predicted."[20] His solution to this problem: "I had attempted to explain how the appearance of Christ coincided with the beginning of a new aeon, the Age of the Fishes. A synchronicity exists between the life of Christ and the objective astronomical event, the entrance of the spring equinox into the sign of Pisces. Christ is, therefore, the 'Fish' (just as Hammurabi before him was the 'Ram'), and comes forth as the ruler of the new aeon."[21] Jung here shows that he not only takes a pseudo-scientific approach to astrology, but he gives it a historical and religious significance. It becomes a key interpretive concept for important aspects of life.

HOW ASTROLOGY WORKS

The main principle of astrology is: "as above, so below." Any event in the heavens affects earthly existence. The fundamental assumption behind this theory is monism: all of reality is a single whole, and everything affects everything else. Astrologers believe they discovered some of the laws that explain how the world and human personalities work. For a fee they will apply their knowledge to help you discover your personality and your future as part of the one, whole world.

The first step is to locate all the planets on a particular day by looking it up in an ephemeris, a table that identifies the location of the planets in relation to the constellations of the zodiac. Each planet has a particular kind of influence on each person at the moment of his or her birth. The basis for explaining the nature of these planetary influences rests on ancient pagan belief from Babylon and Greece that gods inhabit, control, and move the planets. The personal characteristics of each god—Mercury, Venus, Mars, Jupiter, and Saturn—determine the kind of influence its planet has on a person.

Most of the characteristics ascribed by astrologers to these planets are the same ones noted by Ptolemy in his astrology book *Tetrabiblos,* A.D. 140. Of course, the planets newly discovered in modern times—Uranus, Neptune, and Pluto—have unknown influences. On the other hand, this lack of knowledge lets each astrologer make up his or her own interpretation of these planetary influences. As my Bahai astrology teachers often said, "Where there is confusion, there is possibility."

The next step is to examine the aspects of planets, which means their relationship to each other. Opposition means that planets are found in opposite signs of the zodiac, while "conjunction" means they are in the same zodiac sign. Other angles can be good or bad aspects. Bad aspects are associated with angles containing the bad numbers 2, 4, and 8, while good aspects come with angles having the numbers 3, 5, 6, 12, especially 3. The "good" or "bad" evaluation of these aspects depends on an astrologer's interpretation of ways the characteristics of the gods of the planets—Venus and her husband Mars, for example—interact. Opposition between the planets is apparently fine, while conjunction is better for others. This level of interpretation shows how closely astrology is tied to its pagan origins.

The zodiac is an imaginary circle around the ecliptic of the earth's annual trip around the sun. Astrologers artificially divided it into twelve equal sections of thirty degrees each, with each delimited by a constellation. However, note that according to astronomy, the constellations are *not* equally distributed about the ecliptic. The following shows the *actual* degrees of each constellation on the ecliptic:

Aries	24.5	Virgo	44.0	Aquarius	22.5
Leo	35.5	Capricorn	29.5	Cancer	20.0
Sagittarius	33.5	Gemini	28.5	Scorpio	7.0
Taurus	36.5	Libra	23.0	Pisces	37.5[22]

This unevenness means the month ascribed to each "sun sign" in newspaper columns does not correspond to the easily verified scientific data about the real amount of time the sun lies within the constellations. This, too, is a bogus element in astrology.

Astrologers believe that each sign of the zodiac is ruled by a planet. Only nine planets orbit the sun, of which the ancients knew only seven (including the moon), so some planets rule more than one sign. Since Mars, the warrior god, ruled Aries, an aggressive sign, one would expect military leaders to be born when Mars is in Aries. However, the astronomer Gauquelin has shown that no such correlation exists. In fact, a number of studies, including Gauquelin's study of twenty-five thousand people, showed that no occupations correspond to birth signs, whether sun signs or ascendents. The distribution of careers throughout the zodiac fits patterns of chance, not astral determination.[23] Further, in the absence of any tradition about the roles of the new planets, astrologers can invent ideas about their alleged influence within the constellations, which they do.

The art of the astrologer seeks to understand the role of the planets in relationship to the zodiac and to each other. The hundreds of factors in each horoscope make interpretation extremely complex. The pop astrology in the newspapers only gives "sun signs," that is, the influence of the sun's location in the month of one's birth. An authentic horoscope requires much more information and is done by a skilled interpreter. Therefore, people will feed in the necessary data and then command a computer to print out their horoscopes, or consult a professional for a reading at anywhere from twenty-five to seven hundred and fifty dollars per session. This can be expensive for the customer and lucrative for the practitioner.

All of this is to say that astrologers must be very intelligent to cast charts and would be worth every penny paid to them, if only there were any truth to the basic claims of astrology. However, since the basic scientific data disproves the possibility of doing astrology, every penny spent on it is wasted.

HISTORY OF ASTROLOGY

Astrology probably had its beginnings in the third millennium B.C., in Sumer, though its earliest evidence is on clay tablets from second millennium Babylon. The Mesopotamian ziqqurats, clay-brick temple towers like the Tower of Babel, were built as platforms to observe the stars and cast astrological charts. At first astrology only foretold the fate of the monarchy and the state, not of individuals. Ancient Mesopotamian cosmology is still the basis of present day astrology. Shamash the sun-god and law-giver ruled the day, while the moon-god, Sin, ruled the night. They moved along the heavenly equator, named after another god, the "Way of Anu." Hence, the influence of the sun and moon along the ecliptic goes back to Babylon.

The Egyptians practiced their own system with thirty-six divisions in the sky instead of twelve. Their year had thirty-six weeks of ten days each. This Egyptian system corresponds to neither the Babylonian nor the sixth century B.C. system used in India.

During the Hellenistic period (fourth to first centuries B.C.), the Greeks combined Egyptian and Babylonian astrology with their own mathematics and astronomy, thereby forming the system presently used in the West. In addition, the Greek democratic ideal led them to cast charts for individuals, as is still practiced today.

The Chinese developed an independent tradition of astrology with twelve months. The Druids of ancient England built Stonehenge as a sort of astronomical observatory, perhaps for astrological reasons, though the exact purpose is not clear. The Mayans had a calendar and astrological system, and they observed the stars from their pyramids. The monist belief that the heavens directly influence earth ("as above, so below") appears the world over. However, none of these systems coordinate with the others. They all are mutually exclusive. How can they all be right? In fact, how can any of them be right if the basic astronomy is not scientifically sound?

CONVERSION FROM THE CLUTCHES OF THE STARS

I was only mildly disconcerted when my astrological activity scandalized some evangelical and Catholic charismatic friends and students. But it was bothersome. Since my goal was to help others, I did not easily comprehend their rejection of my "science."

Then I started to notice that when interpreting people's charts, I watched their faces for approval or disapproval of my analysis. This was like my father, a used car salesman, reading his customers' faces. I would correct and adjust the analysis according to the way I read their faces. I did not like my dishonesty, slight and unconscious though it might have been.

The astrologers' books, like Dane Rudhyar's, admitted that the astrological system in common use had been inaccurate for two hundred years. At first their idea that the zodiac is a metaphor of human psychology pushed the facts of astronomy out of my mind. However, I eventually had to reexamine the scientific bases of astrology, since science had been my only justification for its practice.

Theology and spiritual books, in particular, *The Holy Spirit and You*, by Dennis and Rita Bennett, forced me to rethink my whole attitude toward astrology and everything else of the occult. Though I now value the theological reasons far above the scientific, the latter began to change my attitudes before I accepted God's Word on it.

The simple truth is that science denies astrology any basis in fact. For instance, the belt of the zodiac has altered its former relationship to the earth. Everyone's astrological sign is different from the claims of the newspapers and books.

> As the earth moves in orbit around the sun, the sun seems to follow a path in the sky called the ecliptic. This is known as the belt of the zodiac, eighteen degrees wide. The Babylonians and the Chinese divided it into twelve parts, each marked by a constellation of stars known as a sign. The Egyptians had thirty-six divisions. Not only are the constellations arbitrarily designated configurations, but the procession of the earth's axis slipped the earth's relation to the sign thirty degrees West, about one whole sign out of alignment.[24]

This means that everyone needs to change the astrological sign under which he or she was born. Whatever date the newspaper gives for your sign, move it back one whole sign, because that, in fact, is your real sign. The proof lies in any map of the universe that gives the dates for the entrance of the sun into the twelve constellations of the zodiac. Check the dates when the earth actually enters each sign and compare those dates with the ones given in any newspaper. All of them are one sign or month off!

Once I returned from a swim on the beach to find a

three-year-old boy charming two women in their early twenties. He had them wrapped around his little finger. They asked him about his astrological sign and, amazingly, he knew it! After the boy went off to his daddy, I briefly explained the precession of the earth and the incorrect identification of everyone's astrological sign. One woman said, "Like, I knew I had a lot of Capricorn in me!" Some people are terrific at preventing facts from getting in the way of their ideas.

Another scientific criticism is that no gravitational pull is strong enough to influence babies at birth. The doctor who delivers a baby has one hundred and eighty-five thousand times more gravitational pull than the moon, and this book held at arm's length has a billion times the tidal influence of Mars! Neither can the radio waves of the planets offset the radio and television waves that bombard us from local communications towers and satellites.[25] Nevertheless, people like Shirley MacLaine claim: "A spiritual guide had told me that the energy one inherits on one's birthday is very powerful, because the sun and its complementary planets are emitting the same aligned energy that they did the moment you were born. You 'own' that energy. It is yours to use in projecting whatever you want of it for the following years."[26] Astrology does not explain the greater influence of the moment of birth over the moment of conception. Obviously, horoscopes focus on birth because there is a definite date; whereas, calculating the date of conception is guesswork at best.

Another myth is lunacy—the influence of the full moon on human behavior. Nurses at emergency rooms, workers in mental hospitals, and police sometimes feed popular belief in lunacy by claiming that more people act up when the moon is full. They may not be able to explain it, but they notice the crazy behavior of patients and criminals. A Miami psychiatrist, Arnold Lieber, wrote *The Lunar Effect*[27] to demonstrate scientific evidence in support of the moon's effect. Since the human body is eighty percent water, the gravitational pull of the full moon must influence behavior through "biological tides." The claims of professionals like nurses, doctors, police, and psychologists, and Lieber's theory seem to explain this lunar phenomenon satisfactorily. Or do they?

In fact, the gravitational pull of the moon does not depend on the phase of the moon. It does not matter whether the moon is full, waxing, waning, or new. Instead, the distance between the moon and the earth determines the tides. Also the alignment of the sun, moon, and earth, taking place every two weeks in either new or full moon phases, makes for greater tides. This simply means that the full moon does *not* cause higher tides and therefore cannot explain higher "biological tides." Lieber's gravitational theory is an inadequate explanation of the facts.[28]

Second, the moon has a negligible influence on the human body. Our weight is a measurement of the earth's pull on the body. The moon's pull is approximately only three parts in a million, about 0.01 ounce on a 200-pound person. This means that the moon can increase such a person's weight through its gravitational pull by only 0.0003 ounce, which is less than the weight of a mosquito. Furthermore, the influence of the moon's tidal force on the blood circulation is about one part in thirty trillion of the blood's weight.[29] Science demands that we discount this negligible effect on our personality.

A third problem with Lieber's lunar theory is that other scientists have been unable to reproduce or substantiate his claims for the social effects of the moon. Other scientific studies showed no correlation between the phase of the moon and murders, admission to mental institutions, births, or even the 28-day menstrual cycle (remember, the moon's phases take 29.53 days, not 28, like the average menstrual cycle). So far, the facts do not support belief in lunacy and other lunar influences,[30] which further undermines astrological theories.

PSYCHOLOGICAL CRITIQUES OF ASTROLOGY

As a test of the psychological validity of astrology, Michel Gauquelin studied astrological descriptions in the computer horoscope industry. He sent in the names of ten friends, but assigned the birth times and places of ten of the worst criminals he could find. One was Dr. Marcel Petiot, who claimed to have murdered sixty-three refugees from the Nazis in occupied France. The horoscope described him as a person of "instinctive warmth... who submits himself to social norms... and endowed with a moral sense which is comforting."[31] Hopefully, the stars will not influence more people to be as warm and noble as he!

Later, Gauquelin made a newspaper offer for a free ten-page horoscope and sent Petiot's horoscope to all one-hundred-and-fifty respondents. Ninety-four percent of those who wrote back to Gauquelin recognized themselves in Dr. Petiot's horoscope, and 90 percent of their families and friends agreed with them.[32] This study indicates that faith in astrology inclines one to accept its results, whatever those results might be.

My friend, the late Walter Martin, explained other psychological fallacies on an audio tape about astrology. A computer programmed for synonyms showed the terms describing the twelve signs mean about the same thing. Of course, astrological portraits are right: they all describe basically the same personalities![33]

An accepted technique for meeting people in singles' bars is to ask about their sign. This is either a clever come-on or a way to turn someone off: "Scorpios turn me on, baby." "Sorry, Charley, Capricorn bores me." Such astrological typing becomes a cheap way to pretend one has a grasp on the mystery of another person. One expects singles' bars to be centers for manipulation, and they should be avoided. Astrological typing of people, with no scientific or psychological basis, is equally prone to manipulation. It, too, should be avoided.

GOD'S WORD ON ASTROLOGY

During my horoscope period, evangelical and charismatic friends called it an occult practice. I countered their religious criticisms by claiming biblical support for astrology. I believed that the magi of Matthew 2:1-2 were Zoroastrian astrologers. They saw a star of a Jewish king in the East, so they journeyed to find him in Judea. However, I had a lot to learn about this story. The star only brought the magi as far as Jerusalem and Herod the murderer, which indicates astrology's limits. Herod then had to ask teachers of the Bible where the Messiah was to be born. The answer had been foretold by the prophet Micah seven hundred and twenty-five years before Christ: the Messiah would be born in Bethlehem (Mi 5:1-2). Only after hearing God's Word could the star continue leading the astrologers to Jesus.

When they arrived in Bethlehem, they worshiped the Lord Jesus in the manger. Like the magi, all astrologers should give up baseless occult practice in order to worship at the feet of Jesus. Gold, frankincense, and myrrh were tools of the magis' trade. They left them with Jesus who could transform them into signs of his kingship (gold), divinity (frankincense), and his saving death on the cross (myrrh for embalming). Every occult tool must be left at Jesus' feet to free us to follow only him as Lord and Redeemer.

Another fact I was reluctant to face is Scripture's explicit condemnation of astrology. Here is the clearest text on the subject (Is 47:12-15):

Stand in your enchantments/ and in the multitude of your sorceries,/ in which you have labored since your youth./ If so you may be able to profit, if so you may terrorize./ You weary yourself with the multitude of your counsels./ Let those who divide the heavens,/ those who gaze at the stars, the ones who know the months/ stand, and save you from that which will come upon you.

See, they are like stubble,/ the fire will burn them;/ they will not deliver their souls from the power of the flame./ It is not a coal to warm them,/ a fire to sit near.

So will they be who you labored with,/ who have done business with you since your youth.

Each shall wander to the path before him;/ there is no one who saves you.

This is hardly our Lord's seal of approval for astrology. Isaiah uses irony to warn against faith in astrology. He addresses the astrologers of Babylon, the homeland of the art. They could not predict their own future with astrology. Only Yahweh, the God of Israel, knows the future and reveals it through his prophets. Rather, the astrologers are like dry stubble about to be consumed by fire.

Another warning against astrology is given in Jeremiah 10:1-3: "Hear the word which Yahweh speaks to you, house of Israel: Thus says Yahweh: Do not learn the way of the nations, and do not be dismayed at the signs of the heavens, though the nations are dismayed at them. For the customs of the peoples are a vanity, for it is a tree he cuts from the woods, the work of the hands of an artisan with an ax." Remember that the ancients believed the gods inhabited the heavenly bodies, so it is quite logical to connect warnings against astrology with the foolishness of idolatry.[34] Jeremiah says that it is a "vanity," that is, the exhaled breath or halitosis. Astrology stinks, so stay clear of it.

In Daniel 2:27-28, King Nebuchadnezzar was about to execute all the wise men, enchanters, and astrologers in Babylon because they could not make known his dream or its interpretation. Daniel explains the problem to the king: "Neither the wise men, nor enchanters, magicians, and astrologers can interpret for the king the secret which the king has asked. However, there is a God in heaven who reveals secrets and makes known to King Nebuchadnezzar what will be at the end of days" (v. 27). The occult cannot reveal authentic knowledge; only God does. Therefore, like Daniel, limit yourself to God's legitimate revelation.

CHURCH TEACHING ON ASTROLOGY

The Fathers of the Church opposed astrology because it was both self-contradictory and irreconcilable with faith in the God of the Bible. How could the stars *and* God both control human destiny? How could humans have free will if the stars determined their personality and future? These criticisms influenced Constantine when he established Christianity as the official religion of the Roman Empire. He made astrology and all forms of occultism illegal and punishable by death. The fourth-century Fathers of the Church—St. Gregory of Nyssa, St. John Chrysostom, St. Basil, and St. Ambrose of Milan—rose to the occasion by providing strong arguments against astrology and the occult.

Probably the most influential Father was St. Augustine, who described his rejection of astrology in Book VII, chapter 6 of his *Confessions*. His wealthy and noble friend, Firminus, was born at the same moment and place as a slave in his house. How could astrology explain one boy's good fortune and the other's servitude? He further asked how twins could have personalities and histories as radically different as Esau and Jacob in Genesis, yet share the same horoscope? Augustine's analysis was: "It was, therefore, perfectly clear to me that when predictions based on observations of the stars turn out to be true, it is a matter of luck, not of skill. When they turn out to be wrong, it is not due to a lack of skill, but to the perversity of chance."[35] St. Augustine concludes with a prayer that shows his total dependence on God instead of the stars: "For, O Lord, though neither the astrologers nor those who consult them know it, by your secret prompting each man, when he seeks their advice, hears what is right for him to hear. For you rule the universe with the utmost justice, and in the inscrutable depths of your just judgement you know what is right for him, because you can see the hidden merits of our souls. And let no man question the why or the wherefore of your judgement. This he must not do for he is only a man."[36]

Throughout the so-called Dark Ages, astrology faded away. Its resurgence followed upon Western Europe's discovery of Aristotle and Muslim scholars who believed astrology to be scientific. St. Albert the Great and St. Thomas Aquinas demythologized astrology and subordinated its influence to God's providence. A scientific approach lasted well into the Renaissance, even though occult practices also increased at that time. For this reason, on January 9, 1586, Pope Sixtus V wrote a constitution condemning all forms of magic, divination, and the occult, especially astrology. For the Catholic, astrology remains forbidden. The 1917 Code of Canon Law also prohibited superstition, the "great variety of unlawful practices which are insulting to God and things sacred." This includes "divination, fortune-telling, magic, witchcraft, or by whatever other name the forbidden delving into the supernatural may be called" (Canon 2178). Astrology belongs within these categories and, though there is a new code of Canon Law, these practices are still prohibited.

Unfortunately, influenced by Jung and Eastern thought, I also became a proponent of the enneagram, a personality typing system with occult origins. Why did I get involved? What was the attraction? We explore those issues in the next chapter.

FOUR

Tell Me Who I Am, O Enneagram!

A FTER FINISHING MY PHILOSOPHY STUDIES at the University of Detroit in April 1972, my best friend and classmate, Mike Sparough, S.J., and I went to Chicago for a home visit. While we were there, we heard that the newest rage at our Jesuit seminary was a course by Fr. Bob Ochs, S.J., about the enneagram (*ennea* is Greek for "nine" and *gramma* means a "line drawing"). On a sabbatical the previous year, he had learned about a system of nine personality types which he found useful in spiritual direction and self-knowledge. Practically every seminarian was in the course and talked about his personality number or the numbers of other people. "Of course, Jerry tries too hard to help you; he's a two!" "Bob scares me sometimes, but don't most eights?" These sorts of comments were commonplace.

THE ENNEAGRAM WORKSHOP

Bob Ochs was about to offer an eight-day intensive seminar on the enneagram early that May, and I wanted to learn what these numbers and personality types were all about.

Did they conform to the astrological types? Would the descriptions help me understand myself and my friends better? I wanted to know! The only problem with signing up for the enneagram intensive was that Mike and I were expected back at our University of Detroit community. On the Greyhound bus to the Motor City, we decided to ask our superior for permission to attend the workshop, and to our surprise he consented. Another tiresome bus ride to Chicago the next day was worth the course and the promise of a new religious experience.

The workshop's opening activity was stuffing small, round black pillowcases for use in seated meditation exercises. We gathered around a large box of cotton batting, while Bob Ochs repeatedly urged us to pack more material into pillowcases. He insisted on extra firm pillows, so we could sit properly in yoga postures. I got tired of stuffing and would have been satisfied with a smaller pillow, except for Bob's insistence.

The rest of that evening and of the course Ochs taught us "the work": a program of spiritual, psychological, and physical exercises to awaken higher states of consciousness and enlightenment.

THE PHYSICAL EXERCISES

"The work" began with physical exercises, like rolling our heads around our necks to loosen the muscles and slowly jogging in place, while we imagined that we were picking grapes above our heads. There were basic yoga postures too. The cobra posture started with lying flat on the stomach, forehead on the floor. Slowly the head was raised and the back was arched, like a cobra raising its head. As we raised our heads we took in a slow, deep breath, then we exhaled slowly as we lowered to the floor. Anyone who really got into it could add hissing sounds. In the lion position, our palms lay flat on the floor in front of our heads, like the Egyptian sphinx. We then exhaled, raised our heads, and opened our mouths as wide as possible, like a roaring lion. Sometimes we just lay on the floor and groaned out loud.

We tried standing exercises in imitation of a tree, where we stood on one foot. The left foot was placed against the inside of the right thigh and both hands were raised above the head, folded as for prayer. The lying positions were not so bad because it is hard to fall when one is already on the floor. However, I struggled mightily to imitate a tree. It took a lot of pulling and tugging at my stubborn left leg before I could make it stay in place on my thigh. I have enough trouble staying balanced on two legs; one leg was impossible. At first I used my two hands and arms the way a tight rope walker uses a balancing pole. Only after much hard practice could I slowly get my hands above my head.

Some positions required us to stand on our shoulders with our legs over our heads. In the candle position, our legs went straight up over our heads with the toes pointed upward in imitation of a candle flame. Those who wanted to add a Christian dimension to this posture could repeat Jesus' saying, "I am the light of the world." The plow was more difficult because it required stretching the legs upward and then bringing them down over our heads with the toes touching the ground. I eventually mastered these two, but I never learned how to stand on my head. I could not do that as a child or a teenager, and I still could not manage it in my twenties. It was embarrassing to see a sixty-year-old Cenacle sister get right up on her head and remain there as long as she liked. That sight was one of the most amazing in the whole enneagram program.

Bob Ochs emphasized that these physical exercises were essential for balancing the physical and the spiritual, though the meditation positions were the most important. He recommended doing them every day in a well ordered program. We took out our stuffed pillows and sat on them to perform the lotus position. This prayer and meditation posture required pulling one leg over one thigh and the other leg over the other thigh. It made the tree and standing on my head look easy. I could not get my knees and legs to stretch or bend that far, try as I might.

Only after much futile effort did Bob say, "Well, some of the yogis state that Westerners are incapable of the lotus position, so try the half lotus." This required one to place only one foot on the opposite thigh, while the other foot could remain below its opposite knee. I never came to the state of enlightenment that made even the half lotus comfortable, but at least I could manage it. The half lotus became the position for meditating on nothingness or the sacred Hindi syllable "om." This was the first time I practiced some of the Hinduism that I had studied in my undergraduate courses.

SPIRITUAL EXERCISES

Bob Ochs taught us a variety of meditation techniques to empty our minds and liberate us from compulsive thoughts. One example was the "burning log." We lay on the floor and imagined that we were burning logs turning into ashes. The goal was to let go of thought and identity and attain "no-mind."

Ochs introduced techniques and concepts borrowed from Sufism (Islamic mysticism). A key idea was the Sufi belief in three interior spiritual centers. The first is *oth*, the green heart center of the emotions. The second is *path*, the red intellectual center located in the head. The third is *kath*, the black center of will located in the lower belly. Meditation on each center could awaken them, a process necessary for attaining enlightenment or salvation.

He related these centers to the movie, *The Wizard of Oz*, in two ways. First, Scarecrow was looking for a brain, which would be the *oth* center; Tinman wanted a heart, the *path* center; and the Cowardly Lion sought courage, which belonged to the *kath* center of the will. Second, Bob mentioned that in Spain the letter "z" is pronounced like a soft English "th." Therefore, *oth* would be the Spanish pronunciation of "Oz," the Emerald City sought by Dorothy, Toto, and friends. I came to wonder whether L. Frank Baum, the author of *The Wizard of Oz,* had secretly been writing a Sufi story to awaken the consciousness of every American child.

Ochs further recommended that we pay close attention to our dreams and waking experiences to help us in the "work." He also suggested that we avoid the use of all drugs, including alcohol, for the duration of the workshop. While drugs can offer an authentic altered state of consciousness (ASC), it does not last long and the drug is toxic to your body. Only at the end of the workshop did I take a drink. I noticed that I could not concentrate during my meditation for a full day. Another experiment with abstinence and then drinking confirmed the results, and I have avoided distilled spirits since then.

Ochs insisted that spiritual discipline demanded complete honesty since all people are liars, especially in regard to their own faults. To help us overcome our dishonest tendencies, he suggested verbal exercises. For instance, "running the reels" meant dividing our lives into five-, six-, or seven-year periods, as we wished, and writing down every memory we had from each period. Other writing exercises came close to "free association" techniques. Starting with questions like, "What's wrong with me?" or "What brings me down?," we would write whatever came to mind.

Bob advised that whenever we felt like filtering out our spontaneous but embarrassing responses, we should especially note them. While we would not be forced to share anything with the other workshop participants, we were not supposed to screen them from ourselves. I used these exercises not only during the workshop but also in my prayer, meditation, and spiritual direction for the next couple years. Through them I came to a more honest acceptance of my faults than ever before, so I placed a high value on them.

LEARNING THE ENNEAGRAM

On the third day of the workshop we learned the enneagram, the nine personalities located on the circle around an inner triangle and hexangle (see figure).

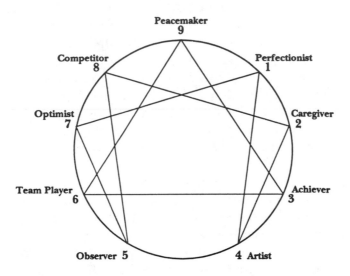

The circle symbolized creation and the unity of life. The triangle represented the trinity, the threeness in God, which is "inside creation." At the nine points where the angles touch the circle lie the nine personality types. Ochs said that these were not merely nine character types but nine divine ideas, the nine faces on the mountain of God, or the nine faces of God within creation. At the same time the nine types are nine devils, personal demons with their own will and intellect. Each type is a neurotic behavior, making it a caricature of a divine attribute, or the "face of God turned

upside-down." During the lecture, I understood these statements to be symbols, not thinking through their theological
ramifications. Only in later years did their inconsistency with
Christianity become clear.

Oscar Ichazo was identified as the man who transmitted
this enneagram to the Western world. Supposedly the Sufis
had invented it centuries ago but kept it a great secret. They
had now decided that it was time to reveal it to the West
through a chosen instrument, Oscar Ichazo. The story of his
role was not clearly told. One version alleged that he had
learned it from Sufis in Tibet, while another said that he got
it from North African Sufis. Like many enneagram enthusi-
asts, I did not question the contradictions of these stories
but remained content to know that I was among the very few
who knew this great secret. Ichazo's background remains
obscure even today, except for an interview with Sam Keen,
an article by Hart and Lilly, and Claudio Naranjo's enneagram lecture.[1] Apparently he prefers this anonymity.

We received loose pages of paper containing descriptions
of each of the personality types. Ichazo called each type an
"ego" as distinct from the essence of personality or the true
self. He gave each ego an uncomplimentary, one-word description which summarized the core problem of the ego's
perversity. Number one was called "ego-resent"; number two
was "ego-flattery"; number three was "ego-go" or "ego-van-
ity"; number four was "ego-melancholy"; number five was
"ego-stinge"; number six was "ego-cowardice"; number seven
was "ego-plan"; number eight was "ego-venge"; and number
nine was "ego-indolent." The descriptions for the types were
written by Ichazo's associate, a psychologist named Claudio
Naranjo. Drawing upon his background in professional psychology, he developed fuller descriptions.[2]

Each ego was described as a poisonous way of being and
relating. No ego could be retrained; removal was the sole
cure. Therefore, the descriptions identified each type's ideal
self-image, chief defense mechanism, the main issue avoided

by each ego, styles of speech, and numerous other factors of personal obnoxiousness.

The descriptions began with the top of the inner triangle, type nine. The "ego-indolent" idealizes the state of being settled and comfortable. Their defense mechanism is narcotization, whether through drugs, sleep, or playing games. Like cartoon characters Dagwood Bumstead or Snuffy Smith, they avoid excitement and work by being lazy. Since problems threaten them, they respond to crises with, "No problem!" Or perhaps they might say, "Don't worry; be happy." They ramble on in monotone voices, putting not only themselves but their listeners to sleep with long, boring sagas.

Next on the triangle is the six, "ego-cowardice." This type idealizes being loyal, especially as it is manifested in obeying law and order. Nonetheless, this is often a way to ignore their own infractions of the law. They are often loyal to an ingroup and see outsiders as threats. Like the Ku Klux Klan hiding behind sheets and hoods, they warn and set limits to what the outgroup might do. They might even break the law to preserve the ingroup. Fear of ambiguity, doubt, and danger dominate their lives. Bravery is the virtue they lack the most.

Three is called "ego-go," a type which idealizes efficiency and external success. Like modern yuppies they compete with the world to acquire the most toys and stuff, overdoing work, play, and expertise. Their chief defense mechanism is identification with the roles they play at work or in society, or overidentification with the company or organization they work for. This defends them from seeing their frailty and lack of success, which they have defined according to impossible norms. They are quite willing to deceive through propaganda if it means that they are successful in convincing someone else of their position. The advertising industry was especially singled out as an example of this type.

Next come the six types of the enneagram's inner hexangle. The "eight" is "ego-venge," so called because it idealizes having power and using it to attack the unjust or the weak. Perhaps the cartoon characters Broomhilda or Hagar the Horrible symbolize this type best. Where threes may avoid failure, eights avoids weakness. Their chief defense mechanism is a denial of weakness in themselves or of innocence in other people. They debunk weakness and injustice in the world, or preach against it. These lusty types grab for power and control, often screaming loudly and bullying opponents to intimidate them.

Number one is "ego-resent." They are perfectionists, angry at the cosmic mess and imperfection. Felix of *The Odd Couple* fame is a classic type one (while Oscar personifies the eight), idealizing perfection and always trying to be good. Such good boys and girls avoid feeling their own anger, yet they deeply resent ignorance, imperfection, and unfairness. Nevertheless, they know that they see the world's problems better than others, so they feel obligated to teach others or give sermons about perfection.

Type two is "ego-flattery," helpers who give what is not needed and flatter everyone in order to earn love. While they appear to be humble, in fact, they are very proud, acting as if they have no needs. When they are not flattering you, they advise you: "Sure you have a broken back, but have some chicken soup that will help you." The comic strip "Momma" characterizes this personality trap well.

Personality fours, "ego-melancholy," are artistic types who feel that suffering is the way to be special in a plain world. They idealize being sensitive, special, or elite. While threes overdo success, the fours overdo emotions, epitomized by the cartoon character Jessica Rabbit, Roger Rabbit's wife. The chief defense mechanism is artistic sublimation, especially through drama. These characters tend to be refined snobs who lament feeling cast into the midst of boors.

Number fives, "ego-stinges," use intellect to avoid sharing personal experience. The ideal is to be wise and perceptive, so fives tend to observe everything without participating in the action. Their chief vice is avarice: they want to know what everybody else is thinking, read all the books, and acquire all the information, like the brilliant but absent-minded professor. Fives learn so much that they can isolate themselves and be stingy with emotions. In groups, they will listen to what everyone has said and then summarize it into clear categories and intellectual structures. Another form of communication for this type is the philosophical treatise.

Sevens are called "ego-plans" because these compulsive optimists avoid the pain of hard work through constantly planning the future. They want everything to be nice and everyone to be okay. They tell stories about nice things or gossip about other people. Instead of being stingy with their experience like fives, sevens are gluttonous for experience. They always want life to be warm and wonderful, so they avoid pain and the heavy side of life. When things get tough, sevens get going.

As Ochs lectured on each type, I made personal notes relating them to my knowledge of the astrological character types. I hoped to unite the two systems and learn how to determine the enneagram types through the horoscope. Ochs discouraged the idea because the enneagram requires each person to choose his or her own type. The stars do not force a person to become one of the nine types. I tried to figure it out anyway, trusting that Carl Jung's idea of synchronicity would show how the systems worked together. Only years later, after having stopped using both astrology and the enneagram, did I learn that Ichazo had connected the two systems.[3]

My next issue was to identify my personal enneagram fixation: to which of the nine compulsions did I belong? I secretly hoped that I would not fit anywhere. Perhaps I was enlightened enough to be beyond all compulsions. However, the exercises which questioned, "What's wrong with me?" and "What brings me down?" showed that not everything in my life was good or beautiful. Running the reels of childhood and adolescent memories brought to mind unhappy scenes and recollections of things I did wrong. These exercises, along with discussions about the nine compulsive types, helped me pick out my fixation. Ochs did not agree with my choice at first, but another student pointed out traits which fit me quite well. From that point on I worked on making myself free of the fixation and its obnoxious qualities.

What is my type? Sorry, but I keep an unlisted number.

Another student doodled while he took notes. His one-page summary, with doodles, was given to us at the end of the workshop. A participant from the Canadian Province of Jesuits apparently photocopied his, as evidenced by its wide circulation around Canada. Six years after the workshop, a Benedictine prior in Wisconsin showed me his copy of that sheet, which a Jesuit had given him in a directed retreat in northern Ontario. When the Benedictine asked me about it, I laughed out loud. Of course, he could not make any sense out of this enneagram summary since he did not know the people named on the sheet, or how the personality descriptions fit together.

APPLYING THE ENNEAGRAM

The enneagram was as exciting as the theology students had claimed. The new self-knowledge and the acceptance of previously denied negative personal qualities challenged me. Furthermore, this system of personality types helped me accept the different ways other people saw reality and acted. My friend Mike was no longer wrong as often. His approach was different because of his compulsion.

Of course, this raised another question: if the nine types are so obnoxious, then should we not help one another by correcting each other's compulsions? In fact, catching someone else's faults was called "chinging." We were allowed to "ching" in a playful way, but like other games it sometimes got out of hand. Unfortunately, I enjoyed "chinging" my friends. I considered it the first bit of enlightenment, but it probably resulted from my enneagram type.

Mike Sparough and I returned to Detroit when the workshop was over. Our classmates were fascinated with our reports about the enneagram. They wanted to know their personality number. We obliged them to the best of our ability, even though days earlier we had promised not to teach anyone else about the enneagram. It was just too tempting not to answer people's questions with insights from the new wisdom we had just acquired. Perhaps it was the belief that we had received secret knowledge about everybody else in the world that made it hard to resist the temptation to teach the enneagram. It was like knowing a joke and telling it often before anyone else did.

A month later in early June, I moved from the University of Detroit to St. Xavier High School (in Cincinnati, Ohio). I was very angry about being assigned to teach in a high school. This had caused my dread at the beginning of my two years of philosophy studies. The Jesuits at St. Xavier were really good men. I just wanted to teach on the college level, not in a high school. I truly felt stuck.

While in Cincinnati, I made a directed retreat at our retreat house in Milford, Ohio. The director had also made Ochs' intensive course, so we used the enneagram material and exercises in addition to Scripture. I sat in the half-lotus trying to feel the *kath* center in my lower belly and repeat, "There is no God but God." I did free association with questions about what annoyed or frustrated me, or what was wrong with me or brought me down or what hid. The director recommended Scripture passages about light (Lk 11:33-36; 12:1-12, 35-69; Jn 8:12 ff.) to show that God would shine on me and make my inner self known to others and me.

The Scripture that had the greatest impact on me was from the Book of Romans: the law in my flesh fought against the law of God. Try as I might, I committed sins, imagined fantasies, and thought ideas that contradicted my desire to love and obey God. On the basis of the enneagram meditations and verbal exercises, I identified my ego compulsion with the law of the flesh. St. Paul's difficulty in freeing himself from his compulsions spoke to my growing sense of moral weakness.

Such honesty with God scared me. He would certainly smite a sinner like me off the face of the earth. Generally, my approach was to put my head under a blanket and hide from God's judgment. By pretending not to acknowledge my faults, yet trying very hard to remove faults I feared to acknowledge, God might not notice them. At this point, I admitted that these pretend games about sin truly did not reconcile me to God or bring me peace of heart and mind. Escape from honesty became intellectually impossible, so I had to surrender to his judgment and punishment, and perhaps his mercy.

The turning point came in praying over these verses: "Wretched man that I am! Who will deliver me from this body of death? Thanks be to God through Jesus Christ our Lord.... Now then there is no condemnation for those who are in Christ Jesus" (Rom 7:24-8:1). Jesus Christ removed God's condemnation of the sinfulness and compulsion that I had dredged up in the various exercises. I could not hide from it nor could I remove it, but Christ could. Tremendous peace and the beginning of joy came to me the more I repeated this text. I sat for hours in the half-lotus position to contemplate Christ's redemption of my soul.

The amazing grace of the retreat was that the more honest I became with God and the more I confessed my sins, the more consolation and peace I experienced. Instead of immediate extermination, God blessed me with more love. I felt more deeply forgiven than ever before in my life. The capstone of the experience was making one of the best confessions of my life.

Months after the retreat I noticed some improvement in my moral and prayer life. I attributed this to the honesty that the enneagram workshop had taught me and to the Lord's grace. These results further fueled my enthusiasm for the enneagram. Yet they contained the seeds for my eventual disillusionment with the whole mind-set of Ochs' workshop. Increasingly, I realized that the grace of confessing to the personal God who treated me as a person was the true work of conversion. Over the next few months of meditating on free-association questions and Oriental prayer techniques, I lost my zeal for them. Instead, the desire for personal union with Christ Jesus exceeded the ideal of an enlightened state of consciousness.

Yet I used the description of my type to catch personal compulsions and taught short courses in it. Despite Ochs' request that we not teach the enneagram for two years, I (and many others) could not resist the temptation to share the secret. Ochs wanted us to integrate "the work" personally before sharing it with others. Yet Ochs himself had taught the enneagram even though, as Claudio Naranjo claims, the participants in his original enneagram workshop signed a commitment not to teach it to anyone else. Naranjo wanted them to use it solely for their personal development.[4]

However, now Pandora's box of personality types is opened and the enneagram industry holds workshops in parishes and retreat centers throughout the world. Many teachers of "the work" can trace their intellectual lineage to Ochs' workshops and courses.

A number of times I was certain about having pegged my friends' enneagram types, but when they looked at the charts, they chose something different. Sometimes I found myself forcing experiences into the categories of my enneagram or limiting personal criticism to those categories, even though people saw other faults in me. It was hard to accept faults that were not part of the enneagram descriptions.

Furthermore, I became increasingly suspicious about the

antiquity of the enneagram in typing personalities when I failed to find it mentioned in any books by Gurdjieff or his disciples. The enneagram figure was there, but the personality types were never mentioned. Admittedly, it was supposed to be secret knowledge, but Gurdjieff's disciples apparently had no difficulty in revealing other secret parts of the teaching and work in their books. Why was there no mention of it?

I gradually stopped consulting my enneagram notes and, like many of my Jesuit friends, ignored the whole thing. Only recently has my interest been rekindled as I have seen the enneagram grow in popularity among Catholics. But my interest has become a matter of serious personal concern because of the scientific questions, social problems, and theological problems the enneagram poses for Catholics and other Christians. These are the questions and problems that I explore in the next chapter.

FIVE

Occult Roots of the Enneagram

WHILE TRAVELING THROUGH the United States recently, I have noticed that an enneagram industry is spreading rapidly, especially among Catholics. Workshops are offered in parishes and retreat houses across this country, often by priests and religious. New books appear, many of them written by priests and nuns. These books teach people how to identify their enneagram types, improve their personality, and pray in "sync" with their type. Yet these books and workshops do not present a consistent view of the enneagram or its types. The descriptions of the personality types vary and sometimes contradict one another. How are people to know which book is correct or which workshop is responsibly taught?

People around the country have asked me about the enneagram because they hear it has an occult background. At first I dismissed their questions because Fr. Bob Ochs certainly did not teach us any occult aspects of the enneagram. In fact, he wanted to relate the enneagram to traditional Catholic mysticism, such as that of St. Teresa of Avila or St. John of the Cross. However, a conversation with Dorothy Ranaghan and reading her booklet *A Closer Look at the Ennea-*

gram[1] forced me to reconsider the possibility that there is an occult background to the enneagram. The books by Gurdjieff's disciples and articles about Oscar Ichazo prove that they practiced occultism and that occultism is interwoven with the enneagram itself. Therefore, I believe Christians need to be aware of the enneagram's occult origins so they can prevent occult traces from infecting their faith in Christ Jesus.

The enneagram entered Western culture through the schools of two men: George Gurdjieff and Oscar Ichazo. Gurdjieff brought the enneagram symbol from the Orient, while Ichazo is responsible for the enneagram of personalities. Much of their doctrine about the enneagram and personalities needs considerable scientific examination. Further, occult influences appear in the teachings of both men. Who are Gurdjieff and Ichazo?

GURDJIEFF AND ICHAZO

Gurdjieff. George Ilych Gurdjieff gave different years for his birth: to some he claimed 1869; his passport had the date December 28, 1877. He told others that an Edison phonograph was playing during his birth, which establishes 1877, since the phonograph was invented that year. He returned to Russia as a millionaire in 1912 and established the "Institute for the Harmonious Development of Man" in Moscow. This was a place to train others to teach the world what he learned in his travels. The Russian Revolution intervened, and he had to move to France.

He learned the enneagram symbol during his travels through central Asia. The Sarmouni and Naqshbandi sects of Sufis (mystics in Muslim societies) taught him the enneagram's numerology and mystical uses. Middle Easterners used the enneagram for numerological divination by searching for the mystical meanings of the decimals .3333...,

.6666..., and .9999..., based on dividing one by three, and of .142857..., which is based on dividing one by seven and contains no multiples of three.² Of course, all divination is forbidden us by Deuteronomy 18:9-14 and other passages. Does this numerology affect the enneagram of personalities? Notice that the first sequence of decimals corresponds to the triangle within the circle and the second sequence corresponds to the six-pointed figure (see figure).

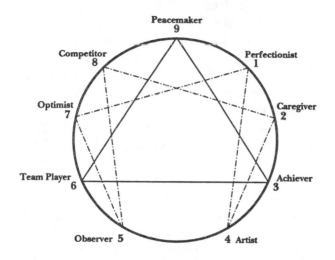

The lines within the circle connecting the points are an important part of the enneagram, indicating the inner dynamics of whatever process it describes.

Gurdjieff believed, "Only what a man is able to put into the enneagram does he actually *know*, that is, understand. What he cannot put into the enneagram he does not know." With it he interpreted processes of cooking food, scientific research, and life itself,³ even though these applications generally appear contrived. Gurdjieff also believed in "demiurgic essences," spirits who are in charge of harmony on earth. Yet he warns in his book *Beelzebub's Tales to His Grandson* that their "work is not necessarily favorable to the liberation of individuals from the cosmic mechanism."⁴

Ichazo. The occult also influenced Oscar Ichazo's life and writings. At age six he began having out-of-body experiences, which led to his disillusionment with the church. He could not accept Catholic teachings on heaven or hell because he had been there and knew more about it than Christ and the church. Later he learned that living in one's ego was the real hell. To gain control of his own consciousness, he studied Oriental martial arts, Zen, Andes Indian thought, psychedelic drugs, shamanism, yoga, hypnotism, and psychology. He joined esoteric groups in Bolivia and Argentina, and traveled to Hong Kong, India, and Tibet to study mysticism.[5] He has reportedly received instructions from a higher entity called "Metatron, the prince of the archangels."[6] Members of his group contact lower spirits through meditation and mantras.

Ichazo is now said to be a "master" in contact with all the previous masters of the esoteric school, including those who have died. The members of his group are helped and guided by an internal master, the Green Qu'Tub, who makes himself known when a student reaches a sufficiently high stage of development.[7] Such spiritistic and occult involvements should signal serious concern for Christians, for whom they are gravely forbidden as mortal sin.

Somewhere in his spiritual search, Ichazo learned the enneagram, perhaps from a Gurdjieff disciple. He then developed a system of nine personality types. The enneagram symbol may go back to fourteenth-century Sufis (though I have never seen the external evidence for this). I certainly have seen no evidence supporting Gurdjieff's claim for its roots in Mesopotamia around 2500 B.C. in my studies of ancient literature and archaeology.

There is no evidence that the enneagram of personality types goes back any farther than Ichazo in the 1960s. Neither Gurdjieff nor his disciples write about it. It was Ichazo who wrote short descriptions of the nine types, employed animal symbols or "totems" for each type, and placed the personality types on the enneagram symbol.[8] For these reasons I call this

Ichazo's enneagram. One of his disciples, Claudio Naranjo, took the next step by placing the enneagram into the context of psychological concepts, like Freud's defense mechanisms.[9]

Significantly, Ichazo's enneagram employs the numerological background of the Sufi decimal-point symbolism in understanding personality dynamics (see figure).

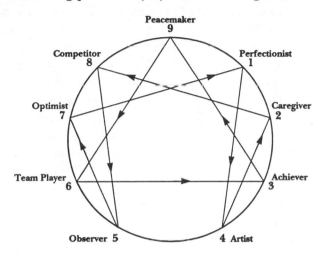

For instance, according to this system, the number one gets worse by following the arrows to type four, four gets worse by becoming like a two, and so on. A person improves by moving in the opposite direction, that is, a one gets better by becoming like a seven, a seven should become like a five, and so on.

Remember that this inner dynamic of the six-point figure and the triangle is based on the numerology of dividing seven into one or three into one, which is rooted in the enneagram's occult origins. There is no reason to accept the geometric design and its numerological logic as an *a priori* basis for determining how people improve or regress. Evidence based on observation of spiritual and psychological growth, without necessary reference to the enneagram or other geometric *a priori* figures, offers a better foundation for spiritual direction.

SCIENTIFIC QUESTIONS

I am concerned about the lack of objective scientific research into the enneagram. I know of eight dissertations on the enneagram, though one of them is from a non-accredited school. Four of them seek to develop testing tools to determine which of the nine personality types fits a person, or to relate it to existing tests like the Myers-Briggs Type Indicator or the Millon-Illinois Self-Report Indicator. Two dissertations study the effects of Ichazo's Arica training, and another studies the enneagram's relation to depth psychology. There is a quarterly publication, the *Enneagram Educator*, and a game, cassettes, and books studying the enneagram. Yet questions remain about certain key points. I believe that empirical testing and verification are needed to answer them. How do we know that there are *only* nine key personality types? How do we know that the types are centered on nine distinct prides or ideals? Can we prove empirically that the nine types found in Ichazo's enneagram are the *correct* nine types? Are the nine types in Ichazo's enneagram authentic character structures? How do we know that the ways of getting worse or getting better are correctly defined by Ichazo's enneagram?

Bear in mind that I am not saying that the information about the types, their descriptions, their regress, or their progress is necessarily wrong. I *am* saying that we do not *know* how correct or incorrect the system is, or if it is right or not. So far, all the evidence is anecdotal—dependent on personal experience—and that is insufficient proof. Psychologists subject their hypotheses to tests which allow the results to be repeated in scientifically controlled situations and criticized by their colleagues and peers. Ichazo's enneagram of personality types should be considered one more hypothesis requiring such scientifically rigorous tests and peer examination.

I personally doubt that the enneagram will stand up to

rigorous examination, but my doubts do not constitute evidence. Publishing this information could help both the scientific community of psychologists as well as participants in enneagram workshops to know whether they are receiving sound advice from an enneagram practitioner.

In fact, because objective study of the enneagram does not exist, there are no norms for deciding who is an authentic or qualified enneagram teacher. No tests, no standards, no board of examination exists, so most enneagram "experts" have that title through self-declaration and workshop advertising. People do not go to doctors and psychologists unless that practitioner is tested and licensed. Should not some similar requirement be made of enneagram teachers, who not only explain what your personality is like but make recommendations about what you should be like? Until such verification of the enneagram occurs, resulting in ways to discern who has enneagram expertise, I recommend that people not patronize the workshops, seminars, and retreats.

SOCIAL PROBLEMS

When I first learned the enneagram of personality, it was the rage of our seminary community and eventually affected the whole province, though to a lesser degree. One recurrent problem with its popularity was its use as a personality shorthand. Knowing the personality types of friends and acquaintances, or speculating about the type of persons unknown to us, became quite common. "I'm a three." "You're a two." "Ones drive me crazy," became typical comments. The enneagram types were tossed around in conversation like astrological signs at a party.

As with any personality typing system, this problem has a number of facets. There is the danger of believing that once we know to which of the nine types someone belongs, we can understand his or her inner drives and compulsive

behaviors. This was supposed to be a strength of the enneagram, since we would better appreciate the real differences
between people. However, it can also shortcircuit authentic
interpersonal relationships. One party thinks he or she
knows more about another party before that person has
chosen to reveal private and intimate information. This
dynamic can make certain devotees of the enneagram
believe that they are in on secrets about other persons,
which, in fact, they can only guess at.

Many of the enneagram books and teachers also use historical characters as examples for understanding the various
types. Hitler is an "eight," the "ego-venge" type seeking
power, while the philosopher Martin Heidegger is a "five,"
the "ego-stinge," seeking wisdom. Yet a supposed strength of
the enneagram is that each person mulls the descriptions of
the types, learns about the types from people who already
know their enneagram number, and then chooses his or her
own place among the ego-trips. But Hitler, Heidegger, and
other dead people did not have the opportunity to identify
their own type. When the enneagram practitioners identify
the personality types of famous people they never knew,
their example encourages their students to do the same with
people they do not know very well.

In our workshop in 1972, certain members of my province were typed without their knowledge. As mentioned earlier, this typing was written into the notes of a student who
doodled during the workshop. The notes were then photocopied in Canada, passed out to retreatants, and years later
reappeared in the Chicago area in the hands of a Benedictine prior. When a priest described in the notes did learn
about the enneagram, he identified himself with a completely different number!

I am guilty of similar misidentifications, which at times I
tried to foist on my friends. In three summers of contact
with enneagram workshop participants, one of my students
was typed all the way around the circle of nine by one devo-

tee after another. He resented the invasion of his privacy and attempt at control by means of supposed knowledge, as well he should have. When the enneagram workshops are opened up to entire parish groups, the same problem will inevitably appear. It is part of the enneagram game.

ENNEAGRAM MYTHS

When we first learned about the enneagram we were told that it was an ancient Sufi personality system just recently revealed to the West through Oscar Ichazo. Much of its authority in our lives depended on its antiquity and the presumed wealth of experience behind it. However, the enneagram literature provides no evidence that it antedates Oscar Ichazo. Palmer[10] and Naranjo[11] stated that the personality system is a creation of Ichazo and Naranjo in the 1960s. It is therefore important to dispel this myth of antiquity and look to scientific verification as its authority. Otherwise, it has no authority except the personal experience of those who give and make the workshops. Personal testimony and provable antiquity are the authorities behind the astrological types, yet these occult, astrological systems are unacceptable because of their lack of scientific support.

Another myth comes from the attempt to relate the enneagram to religious language. Some teachers state that the nine types are the nine faces of God, or that upside-down they are the nine faces of the devil. Apparently this is based on Ichazo's idea that when we were born we lived in our essence. Around age three or four, we developed defenses to cope with society and that process produced our "ego," whose existence is the main problem the enneagram workshops try to solve. Remove the ego and one can return to the essence, which is apparently divine.[12] Ichazo believes that the ego is the Satan in one's life, and living according to the ego is hell. Therefore, it follows that the reversal of the ego, turning it upside down, is divine. This is a myth. We humans are not God. God is infinite being, three persons in one being. God is our Father, revealed by his Son, Jesus Christ, and confirmed by the gift of the Holy Spirit. Jesus our Lord made no mention of nine faces of either God or the devil. I see no need to add an enneagram myth to our faith.

A related myth is that Jesus our Lord must have had all nine personality types perfected within him. One will believe this myth only if one first believes that perfection requires the possession of all nine types. What is the basis for accepting *that* myth? Then we need to remember that the Gospels do not give us information about our Lord's personality type. As a Scripture scholar, I maintain that the evangelists did not intend to give us biographies of Jesus but proclamations of their faith in him. They announced his divinity, humanity, his death and resurrection, and the teachings we need for salvation. It is a mistake to look to the Gospels for information about Jesus' inner personal dynamics. Any attempt to do so ends up creating a myth about him.

One of my former teachers and a fellow student in the 1972 enneagram workshop came to my house for dinner a few years ago. In the middle of a conversation, he suddenly pronounced: "Original sin begins at age three or four." The comment came from out of left field, and I did not have a mental context with which to respond to him. He apparently has been so influenced by Ichazo's idea that we stop living in our "essence" at age three or four that my friend now identifies original sin with the process. This, too, is a myth. Original sin is not an offense committed by each individual or a condition that we grow into. It is each human's lack of sanctifying grace (not essence) which we all inherit from our first parents.

Whenever enneagram devotees make mythic statements, one should feel free to question the myth. Examine their assumptions. See if their theology is orthodox Christian belief or orthodox Ichazo and Gurdjieff belief. In the face of any conflict between the two, opt for faith in Christ Jesus and his church. Remember the warning in 2 Timothy 4:3-4: "There will be a time when they will not endure sound teaching but will gather for themselves teachers who tickle their ear. They will turn away their ear from the truth and will turn to myths."

THEOLOGICAL PROBLEMS

Most of my theological problems with the enneagram workshops are based on my critique of the occult and mythic aspects of the teachings of Gurdjieff, Ichazo, and other teachers. I do not accept Gurdjieff's claim to teach esoteric Christianity;[13] Christianity does not need secrecy or esotericism. Our faith is open to anyone who wishes to examine Scripture and church teaching.

Esoteric religion is usually a cover for a doctrine at odds with authentic Christianity. Nor do I accept Ichazo's denial that there is "any creed or dogma" in his Arica training.[14] He includes many religious and occult items within his system, including the belief that a devotee can only receive the "grace" of getting better when he or she remains a member of the group.[15] In fact, if a student does not meet Ichazo's and the group's expectations, he or she can be rejected. This could lead to becoming "crystallized in ego for all future generations" with no chance of entering pure essence. In other words, non-membership can lead to damnation, according to Ichazo's system.[16] This sounds very dogmatic to me, and since it is unprovable, one must take it on faith.

At the outset, we must reject all contacts with spirits like Metatron, the Green Qu'Tub, and the past masters of Sufism. Nor should we accept Ichazo's use of the Cabala of medieval Jewish esotericism, the *I Ching*, a Chinese divination tool,[17] his astrological connections with the enneagram,[18] or any other occult item. Scripture and the church repeatedly condemn mediumship, divination, familiar spirits, and the like (Lv 19:31; 20:6, 27; Dt 18:10-11; Is 8:19). Likewise, we are sensible to reject Ichazo's belief in reincarnation, out-of-body experiences, or belief in the importance of drugs as a way to begin experiencing higher altered states of consciousness (an idea shared by Gurdjieff). None of these practices is consistent with Christianity.

There are serious theological problems with the notion of salvation in the enneagram system. In general, these ideas are inconsistent with Christianity. Thus, they should not be taught in retreats or parish workshops.

First, the human dilemma, according to Ichazo and Gurdjieff, is not the same as Christian faith. Both agree that humans do much wrong and are trapped in negative patterns. However, the enneagram teachers say that we are born in our essence but fall into our ego trips as a response to society's expectations. Catholic faith states that we are born with original sin. St. Paul says in Romans 5:12, "Therefore, since sin entered the world through one man and through sin came death, as also does death pass to all men, since all have sinned." The offense is not merely the acquisition of compulsions but the lack of sanctifying grace which predisposes us to continue to disobey God. Sin is not an ego trip but a turning away from God, a disobedience by humans with a free will against God's freely given commandments.

Second, Gurdjieff and Ichazo hold contradictory ideas about our free will. On one hand, they deny that we have free will until we attain certain stages of enlightenment, which we gain through the "work" of learning from the enneagram. On the other hand, they teach that we should take control of our own lives to save ourselves.

Catholic doctrine is different. We admit that the human free will is impaired by original sin, but it is not destroyed. We have to make choices, and God our Lord will hold us responsible for them. Otherwise, Jesus Christ's doctrine that he will judge us is utter nonsense. On the other hand, we do not rid ourselves of our sins merely by an act of our will. Jesus Christ died on a cross and redeemed humanity by this free act of God made flesh. We do not even take the initiative to be redeemed; God does. The Father chose to send his Son and the Holy Spirit before we were born.

God chooses to give us the gifts of saving faith, hope for eternal life, and love of God and neighbor. We have the free will to accept these graces and cooperate with them. The Scriptures teach both the existence of our free will and the absolute need of humans to be saved by God. Those who conduct enneagram workshops or retreats must teach these truths in order to remain authentically Catholic.

Finally, the goal of the enneagram is different from the goal of Christianity. Gurdjieff and Ichazo were highly influenced by their travels to the Orient, as they freely admit. They learned there that the goal of meditation and self-work is enlightenment, an altered state of consciousness (ASC) or *nirvana*. One attains these goals through breathing exercises, yoga, meditation, Sufi dancing, the martial arts, and other disciplines and philosophies. People feel called to do the enneagram work to destroy the ego trip described by their number and return to their essence. This is freedom from subjectivity and perhaps the type of dissolution of the self into *nirvana* or *Brahman* that is taught in Buddhism and Hinduism. If need be, one will return in many reincarnations until one gets to one's essence.

Jesus Christ describes the goal of our salvation in a number of ways. We are to be reborn as the adopted children of God (we are not born in the divine nature, however). Our sins are forgiven in baptism, and we become members of the Mystical Body of Christ, his church. He desires that we remain in union with the tri-personal God—Father, Son, and Holy Spirit—for all eternity. We do not try to cease to exist, nor do we seek to dissolve in the infinite divine ocean of nothingness. God loves us and wants us to be with him forever in heaven. He promises to raise us from the dead, to glory if we are righteous or to damnation if we turn from him. This is the future God reveals to us in Christ, the life Christ died to offer us.

CONCLUSION

I have many criticisms of the teachers of the enneagram and some of them are quite serious. I do not exclude the possibility of using some form of nine personality types, if indeed their existence can be proven. I suspect that the enneagram is untrue, but is believed by adherents who have faith in its allegedly ancient mysticism.

The mixture of so many non-Christian elements in the enneagram system raises the need to be very careful about accepting it wholeheartedly. St. Paul instructs us, "Test everything; hold fast to that which is good; abstain from every form of evil" (1 Thes 5:20-21). When we test the enneagram, we use the gospel of Jesus Christ as the norm by which we judge it. We do not use the enneagram to test the truth of the gospel. The enneagram is a mixed bag and does not bestow eternal life. Only Jesus our Lord does.

SIX

The Way out to Jesus

W HY DID I TAKE THE ENNEAGRAM WORKSHOP? Why were spiritual issues so important at the end of my undergraduate studies in philosophy? Like others embarking on a spiritual search, a career and vocation crisis stimulated exploration in mysticism.

Before graduating from the University of Detroit, my Bahai World Game friends invited me to teach Bucky Fuller's ideas at a small Franciscan college near Detroit. My Jesuit superiors had other ideas and ordered me to accept what I thought was an awful assignment—teaching freshman religion at St. Xavier High School in Cincinnati. The director of studies told me that his decision was partly based on my need to learn religious obedience.

I was offended and angry for a number of reasons. Why did *I* need to learn obedience? Shoulder-length hair and smoking a few marijuana joints did not mean I needed obedience training! Besides, countercultural values about education and discipline had real merit. Why should teachers impose the strictures of sitting in rows of desks or rote memorization of dogmas upon fresh, open, and creative adolescent minds? Why should Jesuits run a daycare center for bourgeois boys? Besides, I did not even like high school boys. Why not teach World Games and make a difference in the way the whole world works? Training a few boys in religion could hardly change the world, but rethinking the whole world system would.

I asked the director of studies for permission to get a masters degree in systems analysis and design in an architecture program. He rejected that idea too. Feeling desperate, I almost asked to go to our mission school in Katmandu, Nepal. Not quite that desperate, however, I restrained myself.

This choice between something I loved and something I hated, forced me to decide about my vocation as a Jesuit. God our Lord gave me the grace to pray about this situation. Despite the weird pathways of prayer I took, God opened me to deeper conversion.

THE ENNEAGRAM'S WAY TO ENLIGHTENMENT

Bob Ochs' meditation principles and exercises were meant to free us from the ego compulsions of our enneagram types. Their goal was spiritual enlightenment—an inner state of consciousness above normal, everyday ways of thinking. Removing or destroying the old consciousness was necessary to reach new awareness, which he identified as *nirvana* (a Buddhist term for enlightenment) or as *satori* (Hindu term for enlightenment). His first exercise called for shutting one's eyes and imagining oneself as a burning log turning into ash (an apt symbol for the desired transformation).

Ochs felt an urgency for attaining the enlightened state of consciousness. The serious need for *nirvana* was shown in the story of Buddha, who as a young man, saw a house whose roof was on fire. He ran to the window and warned the inhabitants. They only asked whether the weather was warm and sunny or cool and rainy. The story showed how the mundane concerns of everyday consciousness blocked out awareness of the dangerous spiritual state of everyday consciousness. People will seek *nirvana* only when they feel the heat of their own hell. Lack of awareness of the hell they inhabit *is*, in fact, their hell. Realizing their hellish consciousness becomes purgatory. Awareness of one's spiritual state determines whether it is damnation or the process of purgation. Therefore, you should become aware of your hellish compulsions in order to transform life from hell into a cleansing from evil. Doing spiritual work changes the nature of spiritual reality.

Ochs stated happiness is not beyond reality. It is reality. Instead of the door to happiness opening out, it opens back. So to be happy, just step back to your own reality. Instead of looking outside oneself for happiness, look within. Create a better reality by getting the right state of consciousness. This sounded sensible, so I tried to alter my reality and become happy by doing physical and spiritual exercises.

A key exercise called "no-thought" sought to free the mind of all ideas and desires and allow a new consciousness to take root. It consisted of letting go of thoughts, even the effort of trying to let go. When ideas entered the mind (as they invariably did), you were to let them disappear rather than drive them out. Each day "no-thought" was the prelude to other exercises in order to open my mind to whatever might happen next (similar to centering prayer today).

Integral to many of the exercises was the Sufi system of body centers—the head center, *path*; the heart center, *oth*; and the belly center, *kath*. *Kundalini yoga* had a similar system of seven consciousness centers called *chakras*. At the base of the spine slept the kundalini serpent. Yoga meditation awakened the serpent, and progress in yoga helped the serpent crawl through each *chakra* center. Moving up the spine awakened the consciousness of each center until the practitioner attained enlightenment. While the Sufi system omitted the serpent, entering the three centers through meditation was part of expanding one's consciousness.

One exercise for activating the *oth, path,* and *kath* centers was a meditation on Ravel's "Bolero." Everyone laid on the floor in a darkened room and closed their eyes. Next they divided Ravel's music into three parts, each corresponding to a consciousness center: the repeated three note series should be heard in the *path* (head); the melody in *oth* (heart); and the drum beat in the *kath* (belly). A second exercise, called "refueling," was a breathing exercise to activate the *kath.* First, you were to feel the *kath* center in the belly. Then with your arms raised in the air, you counted to fifty with each breath.

A third exercise to enter the centers began by imagining *kath* as a cauldron of water or a dark lake. Next *path* (the head) was pictured as an open chalice into which fell rain from heaven. With each inhalation, water filled the chalice of the *path* center. It overflowed into the dark lake of the *kath* (belly) with each breath. This showed that the water which comes from heaven is the same as the water in the lake of my *kath*, meaning that heaven and earth are the same. Such an exercise shows the tendency toward experiential monism, feeling the oneness of the world, which characterizes the New Age Movement.

Over the following months, I tried to enter the *kath* center as often as possible. This was the way to become centered and reach enlightenment.

Another important spiritual goal was freedom from the personal compulsions revealed by the enneagram. Freedom from the ego type meant a return to one's essence, that state of consciousness that existed prior to choosing ego at age three or four. Ochs told us not to do the compulsion, to not let it happen. Perhaps there would be no changes at first, but soon virtues would replace compulsions with freedom from the ego. The very attempt to exercise one's will helped to increase the ego, so just let the compulsion not happen.

FACING THE NEGATIVE

A way to find freedom from the ego type was Och's advice to take the "bad trip," examining every inner negative experience. Letting go of one's self-image would enable a person to see the demon that possesses the ego. Seeing the demon would make one fear it. People do not fear enough the madman within, that internal foreign body accepted in early childhood. Only if people fear the demon will they ever flee it and reach the level of personal "essence" or enlightenment.

Some exercises took us on the "bad trip." For instance, a form of free association posed certain questions, and the first answer that popped in the head was written down. Theoretically, the superego (to borrow from Freud's terminology) maintained a self-image preventing one from accepting negative personal qualities. Repeating the questions and writing whatever answer came to mind could penetrate the superego's editing and filtering process. Eventually, unflattering truths would break through, forcing self-acceptance. Once these truths were known, freedom from them through meditation and a change of consciousness was possible. Some examples of the questions and answers I wrote are:

"What brings me down?"
- Being ashamed of my body.
- Feeling pain while sitting in the lotus position.
- Not being able to stand on my head.
- Trying to act like I am an enlightened person, wearing the mask of a guru or expert on spiritual things.
- Not meditating on Christ our Savior.
- Not concentrating during "no-thought" meditations.
- Not being able to admit my faults to others.
- Remembering unenlightened actions.
- Resenting St. Xavier High for hiring me.

- Wanting people to know that I feel shafted about having to teach high school.
- Not wanting to bother with the problems and questions of adolescents; they are not my issues.

"What annoys me?"
- People making fun of Buckminster Fuller.
- Friends making fun of my attempts to meditate.
- Being told by a priest in Detroit that if I did not want to go teach high school, I should leave the Jesuits.
- Brother Jack who thinks no one is a good Jesuit unless they succeed in a high school.
- Other Jesuits who think I will someday come around and actually enjoy teaching in the high school.
- A little kid on a street making fun of my big nose as I walked by.

"What is wrong with me?"
- I am vain about my appearance.
- I am afraid of nature—birds, animals, insects.
- I tell people about my new knowledge of meditation so that they will think I am cool and "with it."
- I want to study World Game in order to be a priest aware of what's happening in the world and "with it."
- I want people to love and respect me rather than Christ who loves me and dwells within me.
- I separate God and myself, instead of turning my whole life over to him.
- I compulsively spread the good news of meditation, but I fear not continuing it myself.
- I am not able to meditate without distractions.
- I want others to perceive me as odd, different, and safely kooky, just so that they will stay interested in me.
- I envision myself as being Bob Ochs' greatest disciple

and most "together" follower. I don't want to settle for less.

- I do not want to admit that anything is wrong with me.
- I fear that no one would like me if they knew all that was wrong with me.
- I feel entirely alone because of my sinfulness, unlovable by anyone, including God.

A similar exercise called for imagining the voice of one who knows everything and speaks the sentence: "Give up your preconceptions and surrender to your destiny." One wrote whatever came to mind with each repetition. Here are some of my reactions:

- The person saying this to me is preaching without helping me.
- I need to give up my preconceptions and surrender to my destiny.
- "You have to give up your preconceptions and stop trying."
- This all-knowing person knows my destiny and would not have me surrender to it unless it was good.
- I need to give up preconceptions about St. Xavier High.
- I need to give up preconceptions about being a good boy.
- I am good only at maintaining the facade that I have built up to fool myself.

Ochs suggested saying every imperfection out loud, adding, "... and that is perfect." Admission and acceptance of imperfections transforms one's consciousness about defects, aids in self-acceptance, and actually changes the defects. Upon completing meditations on sin, I said, "I did these things and that is perfect." The reason to confess sins disappeared when everything was already perfect, so I neglected sacramental reconciliation for a while.

PERSONAL REFLECTIONS

I zealously practiced these exercises to expand my consciousness. On occasion, I used marijuana as an aid in mental expansion. Ochs had said hallucinogenic drugs were conducive to expanding consciousness on a short-term basis, so long as the user realized that all drugs were toxic and therefore dangerous. The risk could be worth taking, though. During the workshop itself, I ceased drinking alcohol because it interfered with my ability to concentrate during the meditations. After the workshop, I reinterpreted the drug experience as a spiritual aid for occasional use, along with meditation.

During marijuana highs, the *kath* center felt more attainable than in sober moments. Marilyn Ferguson frequently recommends drugs as a vehicle to enter the new consciousness. "Psychedelics" are a "technology" to induce "deep inner shifts."[1] She also writes, "The revolution of the 1960s had planted the seeds of apocalypse; the psychedelic drugs, however abused, had given a visionary experience of self-transcendence to a sufficient number of individuals, so that they might well determine the future of human development—'not a Utopia, but a collectively altered state of consciousness.'"[2]

I evangelized family and friends with the good news about the enneagram and meditation, the greatest spiritual discoveries of our time. Everyone had to hear about it—from me, if possible. I had a sense of being on the inside of a new wave of spiritual energy and power for the good of all humanity.

Meanwhile, the day of reckoning with my new assignment to St. Xavier High approached. In early June I packed my belongings, caught a ride with another Jesuit to Cincinnati, and moved into St. Xavier High. Having already decided that I would hate high school ministry, I was miserable from the start. Not wanting to enter into the world of high school teachers, I had little to say at meals. The chairman of theology gave me a religion textbook to prepare over the summer for the fall freshman class. How disappointing to teach dumb freshmen, instead of college students!

Leaving the high school to make my retreat was a relief, even if only after one week. My retreat director had made Ochs' enneagram workshop when I did. His familiarity with the enneagram and the Oriental meditation techniques would help me continue the spiritual work begun six weeks earlier. Honest examination of my compulsions, along with calming yoga and Zen, were the order of the day. They could all be integrated into a relationship with Jesus Christ and St. Ignatius' Spiritual Exercises. All spirituality was really one anyway, so why not join East and West?

THE RETREAT: A POINT OF CONVERSION

The retreat began slowly with exercises of entering the *kath* consciousness center and repeating the phrase, "Nothing is urgent with God," or "There is no God but God." Other exercises aimed at discovering the "bad trips": negative personality traits, habits, and memories from different stages of life, childhood through early adulthood.

For hours I asked questions like, "What frustrates me? What is wrong with me? What annoys me? What brings me down? What do I hide? Why is criticism such a threat to me? What prevents me from seeing others' points of view?" Page after page of my journal was filled with spontaneous answers to these questions in the first five days of the retreat.

About the fourth day, I imagined myself encased in a shell, all dark on the inside. Walking into the sunshine filled the shell with light, exposing my whole interior life. What would people think of me if they knew my insides? Repeating John 8:12, "I am the light of the world," helped me get a sense of Christ as the light filling me. Later meditating on Luke 11:33-36, "Take care, therefore, that the light which is in you is not darkness," triggered two reactions. First, a need to be more open about my inner life and let others help me grow. I was afraid to expose weakness, sin, and failings for fear of rejection. Yet unless I revealed my faults to God, myself and other people, a public revelation would be made on my way to hell. Letting God know me could preclude the exposure of my sins and their deserved punishment.

Second, Scripture began to influence my prayer more. Meditating on Luke 12:35-59 and Matthew 25, on the final judgment and the manifestation of all deeds, stirred up fear of God and his just judgment. Once I imagined John the Baptist crying out that I was a hypocrite, a whitened sepulchre full of dead man's rot. This got me to do "bad trip" exercises, probing my psyche by repeating questions and spontaneous answers. I wanted to free myself of every single compulsive ego trip.

However, meditating on John the Baptist did not convert me. Something was missing. While John appeared to be a very "centered" person, this did not satisfy me. A change in the direction of the retreat, and the rest of my spiritual life, occurred when I pictured Jesus coming toward me.

Not having very deep faith in Christ's power to save and convert me, I tried to perfect myself before coming to him. I prayed, "Lord, I want to believe you are God, but I only believe it a little bit. Help me to believe that you are not only another man or some prophet but God the Son. Lord, I believe, help thou my unbelief!"

At first I started thinking of Jesus as a deeply centered man, living in his essence, totally free of ego trips. Then I imagined the whole universe, everything in creation, as existing in Jesus. Maybe the whole universe could forgive me for my failures. But this thought gave me no peace either. It was too vague, too impersonal. The universe cannot speak or think, yet alone forgive.

So I prayed again, "Lord, I believe, help thou my unbelief. Help me to believe you are truly God, able to forgive my sins." Our Lord Jesus answered that request more wonderfully than I could imagine as I prayed more and more with Scripture.

Scripture Was Key. My director suggested some New Testament passages on God's forgiveness. I chose the two versions of Jesus' call of Matthew (or Levi) the tax collector (Mt 9:9-13; Lk 5:27-32), which end with Christ saying, "I have not come to call the righteous, but sinners to repentance." I caught myself unconsciously substituting "perfection" for "repentance," an error learned from yoga and Zen. Jesus did not require sinners to become perfect or enlightened before forgiving them. As Jesus says in Matthew 9:12, "It is not the healthy who need a physician but the sick."

Christ does not require people to be psychologically whole or spiritually enlightened before they approach him. That is like someone polishing his or her teeth before going to the dentist in order to get the dentist's approval instead of professional help. The meditations on myself, my compulsions, and faults were attempts to straighten out my mind and earn the right to God's love. Christ, on the other hand, approached the tax collector and his sinner friends to accept them as they were, before they were enlightened, freed of ego trips, or living in their essence.

The woman caught in the act of adultery (Jn 8:1-11) showed the contrast between her accusers and Christ. I feared the accusers who could humiliate and stone me once they knew my failures and sins, like the woman who not only had to endure impending death but the shame of public exposure. However, the Lord Jesus protected her from the death penalty by unmasking the accusers to be as sinful as she. Furthermore, he did not condemn her. Perhaps Jesus does not want to condemn or shame me either. Perhaps he even loves me.

When John the Baptist met Jesus he cried out, "Behold the Lamb of God who takes away the sins of the world!" He clearly didn't mean that Jesus was cute as a lamb or had wooly hair and a beard. How was Christ the Lamb of God connected to the removal of the sins of the whole world?

Then I remembered the Jewish scapegoat, on which the high priest would lay hands and confess the sins of the nation. When this goat was driven into the wilderness, the sins went with him and died out in the desert. Jesus is the Lamb on whom we sinners place our sins. He takes our sins upon himself so that they die with him when he dies on the cross. Jesus' power to remove sin does not depend on our states of consciousness or psychic powers, but on his sacrificial death. The death of God incarnate allows sinners to accept responsibility for wrongdoing, no longer denying culpability out of fear of divine condemnation. Rather, the more honestly we disclose sin to God, the more completely he forgives us.

Saved by Grace. During the last three days of the retreat, prayer came more easily. Seven or eight hours of prayer with the Gospels and Romans 7-8 were easy since God granted me a lot of peace. St. Paul's words ministered some of the greatest graces that I have ever experienced on retreat. The Holy Spirit focused my attention on short sections of Romans 7-8 over many different prayer periods, showing that St. Paul's struggle with his fleshly self applied to my life.

Paul's "law in the flesh" that makes him do "that which I do not want to do" (Rom 7:14-16) sounded like the ego type or inner "devil." This inner compulsion wars against the spirit by making a person do things he or she does not want to do. The spirit may desire to do good things, like obeying God's commandments, but compulsive behavior brought one to break the commandments.

"Wretched man that I am! Who will rescue me from this body of death?" (Rom 7:24). I wanted to live a perfect life, but I could not. I wanted to obey God's law, but I could not. Like Paul, I felt wretched. I could feel Paul's frustration at personal failure and made my own the question, "Who will rescue me from this body of death?" Perhaps sin would govern my whole life. Until death, compulsive behavior would make me follow my ego desires, never reaching perfection of consciousness. Who could rescue me from all this?

St. Paul pointed the way out in Romans 7:25: "The grace of God through our Lord Jesus Christ!"[3] God could save me, though I am an unenlightened sinner subject to compulsions. God is more merciful than I assumed. My sense of his mercy was vague, but I was assured that Jesus Christ could save me. I did not have to make myself completely whole, perfect, successful, helpful, wise, or meet any other ego ideal. Christ could forgive me of every sin. He came precisely to save sinners, as the gospel proclaims. Tremendous peace came as I prayed over these verses.

"Therefore, there is no condemnation for those who are in Christ Jesus" (Rom 8:1). St. Paul did not base his confidence on his insight or knowledge. Rather, humans are free from condemnation because Christ died on a cross and rose from the dead, gloriously transformed. *That* gives confidence that we are free from condemnation for sins. Jesus Christ, truly human and truly God, is an infinite sacrifice, a sin offering, for our sins. I felt, as did St. Ignatius and St. Francis of Assisi, like the worst sinner in the world, not deserving God's love. However, Christ is infinite and so is his sacrifice; no sin committed by a finite human being could overpower Christ's sacrifice on the cross.

Arrogantly, I had regarded *my* sins as too much for God's forgiveness. I had to make myself perfect before God would bother to forgive me. That was all wrong. God gives the faith and grace to respond to the call of faith in Jesus, making salvation possible. Jesus does not demand perfection before granting faith. He already loves us and always has, so he is more eager to give saving faith than we are to accept it.

"For what was impossible for the law, which was weak through the flesh, God, having sent his own Son in the likeness of flesh of sin and as a sin offering, condemned sin" (Rom 8:3). Again, my attempts to live the law of God proved futile. I was not strong enough to fulfill it. Since I could not obey the Law, it was unable to transform me. However, by sending Jesus his Son, God could and would make good my faults. Though I am a sinner, God sacrificed his sinless Son as a sin offering for my sake. In this God proves that He loves and saves me. These meditations became a greater source of peace and consolation than Sufi theology had ever been.

"For those who are led by the Spirit of God are children of God" (Rom 8:14). If, as St. Paul teaches, we are children of God by adoption, then we do not have to earn the Father's love. The Father always loves his child, no matter what deeds he or she has done. Not even sin changes the fact that the Father has adopted weak humans as sons and daughters and therefore kings and queens in the Kingdom of God. The Holy Spirit leads us, God's adopted children, to ask for forgiveness and life from God. God's own Holy Spirit leads us to the Father, showing that the Father gives even before we ask him.

Praying over this text increased an awareness of my need for salvation. Being perfect did not give the power to be saved. The attempt to find such power hindered progress toward God (though the very struggle to find perfection helped me learn the need for God's grace). Rather, it is the loving God, sending the Holy Spirit through Jesus Christ as an undeserved grace, who *saves* me.

"But we ourselves have the first fruits of the Spirit, and we groan within ourselves, awaiting adoption, the redemption of our bodies. For in hope we are saved" (Rom 8:23-24). Unsuccessful in freeing myself of compulsion, I experienced an inner groaning. Sin, compulsion, and ego still ran my life. Though I desired freedom from them, Paul teaches "we were saved in hope," awaiting the redemption of the body at Christ's Second Coming. Then he will resurrect and glorify our bodies, removing all compulsion and bestowing the true freedom of God's children. For the present moment, we already believe we are redeemed, because of the call of Christ Jesus and our hope for redemption. He begins saving us already and will completely save us at the end of time.

"Likewise, the Spirit helps in our weakness. For we do not know what we are praying for, but the Spirit intercedes with unspeakable groanings" (Rom 8:26). My weakness in the spiritual life was evident. Becoming the wise teacher of the enneagram, yoga, and Zen, full of insight and spiritual knowledge sounded like a nice goal, but I fell far short of it. However, St. Paul calls for dependence on God the Holy Spirit to help us pray. He, being infinite, knows what we need better than we do. Not only can he pray for our truest and deepest needs, but his power to pray is infinitely greater than our own. Therefore, I could trust that he would teach me to pray and grant a gift of prayer when I needed it most:

Who will separate us from the love of Christ? Affliction or distress or persecution or hunger or nakedness or danger or sword? As it is written, because of you we are put to death the whole day; we are accounted as sheep for the slaughter. But in all these things we are more than conquerors through the one who loved us. For I am confident that neither death nor life, neither angels nor rulers, neither the present nor the future nor powers, neither height nor depth, nor any other creature will be able to separate us from the love of God which is in Christ Jesus our Lord. **Rom 8:35-39**

This text beckons one to ask for greater faith and understanding of Christ's unconditional love. No matter what tribulation or distress may come, even if it is teaching high school freshman religion, he loves us. Not even mistakes prevent Christ from unconditionally loving you and me, since infinite and unconditional love is his nature. He cannot love any other way since that would go against his divine nature.

A fitting image of God's love came on the last day of the retreat. Waking at 5:30 in the morning, I dressed and went for a walk. Chirping birds bobbed heads in the grass, hopping away whenever I got too close—like a scene from the hymn, "Morning Has Broken," made popular by Cat Stevens. After walking around for a while, I sat in a chair to wait for sunrise. Buckminster Fuller had said that we carry phrases from antiquated modes of thought, like "sunrise and sunset." In fact, the sun does not rise or set; the earth spins into or out of the sunlight in its daily rotation. I thought about that as I waited for the earth's horizon to spin into view of the sun.

A God of Love. This suggested a new image of Christ, the Light of the world constantly shining on us. He loves us at every moment of our existence, just like the sun is always shining on the earth. Our problem is that we turn away from him, like the earth turns away from the sunlight and faces its own shadow. When we look away from Christ, losing faith and committing sin, we create a shadow for ourselves and stare into it. Of course, life seems dark and bleak then. We speak foolishly about trying to save ourselves by altering or expanding our consciousness, getting into our essence, or some such idea. That is as naive as saying that the sun rises or sets, though we know better.

The good news proclaims Christ's eternal and infinite love, proven by his death on the cross, while we humans were still sinners (Rom 5:6-11). Jesus Christ is truly the "sun of justice arising with healing rays" (Mal 3:20), "the light of the world" who will not let his followers walk in darkness (Jn 8:12). He never ceases shining on us, if we just turn to him, like the earth turning back toward the sun.

The last step I needed to take in the retreat was to make a

general confession of the sins of my whole life, as St. Ignatius recommends in the Spiritual Exercises. In the last retreat conference, Fr. Bollman agreed to hear my confession. Nervously, I confessed the sin of living according to my devil. This devil prevented me from humbly seeing the face of God right-side-up.

This way of talking about sin came right from the enneagram workshop, where Ochs had taught that the egos were devils or the upside-down faces of God. Freedom from the devil would reveal the face of God right-side-up.

Fr. Bollman was nonplused by such an odd confession, so he asked me to mention something specific. This was embarrassing for me. Admitting my faults to myself or to God in private prayer was hard enough to do. Yet it was still insufficient. I needed sacramental reconciliation that included an admission of sins out loud to a priest. On the first Easter, the risen Lord Jesus breathed on the apostles saying, "Receive the Holy Spirit; if you forgive anyone's sins, they are forgiven them; if you bind anyone's sins, they are held bound" (Jn 20:23). How can the apostles forgive a sin unless they hear it spoken out loud by the penitent? No verse in the Gospel exempted me from having to confess my sins, so I did. Confession was embarrassing and made me feel ashamed of myself, but I did it and was glad for it (when it was all over).

Belief in God's love and forgiveness was difficult, but the Sacrament of Reconciliation was the right place to experience it. In making this general confession of my whole life, I found that the more honest I was with God, the more peace and joy I felt. I had expected the opposite. I expected God to squash me out of existence once I admitted being a sinner. However, it was in an honest, open confession that I discovered Christ loves me while I am still a sinner. Clearly, God had a lot more work to do in me, but I trusted that Jesus, the "origin and finisher of our faith," would bring my life to fullness in his time and in his way.

After the Retreat: A New Beginning. When the retreat was over I went to the Bronx for more philosophy studies at Fordham and began reading the high school religion textbook to prepare for fall classes. My prayer life became more regular than it had ever been since the novitiate. I asked to accept Christ's will for me, and I wanted to develop a deeper Christian consciousness.

Yet as much as my retreat centered me on Christ, I did not completely abandon the enneagram, astrology, yoga, or Sufi techniques. I bought yoga exercise books and practiced it every day, though adapting it to scriptural themes. For instance, in the yoga position called the candle, I repeated the verse, "I am the light of the world." In the position called the tree, I repeated Christ's words, "I am the vine, and you are the branches."

I also cast some horoscopes, though it was not as much fun anymore. I started feeling confused about my enneagram type wondering whether I might be a different number than what I first thought. Finally, try as I might, I still did not want to return to St. Xavier High to teach freshman religion.

What remained from the retreat was a sense of God's presence. Even in the various yoga exercises and meditations, I discerned a need for the person of Christ. A hunger for prayer and union with Christ grew, even though I continued some foolish things at the same time. Christ was willing to take time in completing my conversion.

One August morning I sadly boarded the New York subway to begin my journey to Cincinnati. Overdramatizing my plight, I felt like a passenger in a train headed to a concentration camp. The prospect of teaching was dreadful, making me groan whenever I thought about it.

A dream summed it all up: after being thrown off a freighter into the Pacific Ocean on a starless, moonless night, I could not tell if land was five feet behind me or five thousand miles in front of me. I did not know where to go or how to get there. The pinhole of light in that darkness was an absolute confidence that Christ had called me to be a Jesuit. This was a vocation to obey him and my superiors, no matter how I felt. Therefore, I had to go on to St. Xavier and teach as I was told to do. Little did I realize how our Lord's reward would outstrip my obedience. God would not (and could not) be outdone in generosity.

ST. XAVIER HIGH SCHOOL

Bad things happened as soon as I arrived at St. Xavier. First, the theology department chairman was color-blind. As a result, the book he had given me, which I had used to prepare to teach, was the wrong one. It was the sophomore book, which was a different shade of brown from the freshman one. But, of course, he could not see the difference. None of my class preparations that summer were relevant to the freshman course. He apologized; I cried.

Next the principal asked me to volunteer to be the faculty moderator for a group of Catholic charismatic teenagers at the school. As the guy at the bottom of the totem pole, I did not think I had much choice, so I agreed. I knew nothing about charismatics, but most Jesuits end up doing work they know nothing about until they do it. One English Jesuit asked another, "I say, do you know anything about chemistry?" The other said, "Why no; I've never even taught it."

On reflection, this extra-curricular assignment seemed pretty good after all. The boys only wanted to pray for twenty minutes every day before classes started. Though it meant waking up a little earlier, it would motivate me to keep faithful to daily personal prayer. How could I lead them in prayer if I was not doing it myself every day? Also it sounded better than debate, student council, or some other boring activity. Maybe the Holy Spirit's gifts really were active in the modern church, and these kids could show me some new spiritual paths.

I joined the four or five boys daily in a side chapel. Only one of them prayed in tongues now and again, which I did not like. I would try to drown him out by praying louder in English. Also I did not like these otherwise fine kids inviting me to join them at a large teenage prayer meeting on Friday nights. Every week I found excuses because the last thing I wanted was seeing more high school kids on a Friday night.

Things did not go so well in the classroom either. Every Sunday afternoon I would go to my room to prepare classes. Once there I would start to cry because I had no idea what I would teach the students. The textbook I was supposed to use was even more boring than the one I had prepared over the summer. I hated it.

I tried to supplement the class work with Ochs' meditations, like having freshmen lie on the floor and imagine themselves as burning logs turning into ash. They meditated on their *path*, *oth*, and *kath* centers while listening to "Bolero." It seemed so goofy to them that discipline became a real problem, even among first-semester freshmen! For that reason I would return to my room every Friday, dead tired from teaching and cry all over again. The week was usually just as dreadful as I had expected it to be. Nothing worked in the classroom and I had no idea how to improve it.

Every Friday the other Jesuits asked me to go to the school football games. I found sporting events dull to begin with. Sitting at a football game with fifteen hundred adolescents just made a bad deal seem even worse. Usually I found excuses to avoid the games. But by late October, I ran out of them. So when the boys from the morning prayer group invited me to join them at the Friday night group, I accepted. Being with one hundred and twenty teenagers could not be as bad as fifteen hundred teenagers. I had chosen the lesser of two evils.

A young priest, Fr. Richard Rohr, O.F.M., led the group of praying teens. The kids prayed with tremendous enthusiasm, belting the hymns out loud, raising their hands, and shouting glory to God. Even their praying in tongues, a spontaneous chanting in harmony, sounded sort of nice. Perhaps the early church sounded like this when it prayed together. The first hour and a half flew by, and then Fr. Richard began Mass. His marvelous preaching focused on Scripture and the call to make Christ the center of our lives. It brought to mind many of the things I had prayed about in Romans 7-8. The Mass lasted another hour and a half, but it went by quickly too. I loved it and decided to return to the group again.

Every Friday (except for one football game) I went to the Ursuline High School chapel for the prayer meeting. By the third week I thought that perhaps God had brought me to Cincinnati to get involved with this charismatic renewal. I still did not like the high school, and I did not really want to like it. But I resentfully prayed, "Okay, Lord, I accept that you want me here. I don't like it and I don't want to, but I'll stay on." I had been thinking again about a transfer to Nepal. Things had gotten that bad. This time I did not pursue it because I did not think it was God's will for me. Staying at St. Xavier seemed to be.

By December the morning prayer group at St. Xavier had grown to twelve. The guys were good evangelists who invited other students to join us in prayer. Realizing my need for the gifts of the Holy Spirit to lead and properly direct the group, one Friday night I asked the guys to pray over me for the "baptism in the Holy Spirit." This is a release of the Holy Spirit's power to enable a Christian to exercise his or her gifts (see 1 Cor 12-14).

For the first time I spoke with Fr. Richard, who encouraged me to invite the Holy Spirit to give me the gifts of ministry. Fearing some overwhelming experience, I hesitated. I went on with it because I could no longer depend on personal strength. Quietly, the students laid hands on my head and prayed. No powerful emotion, no deep joy, or other strong feeling came to me. A quiet assurance of our Lord's anointing to lead the prayer group calmed me.

A number of important changes followed this experience. First, prayer became still more Christ-centered than before. The Jesus Prayer, as presented in the book, *Way of a Pilgrim*, helped me to call on Jesus throughout the day. While teaching, going for a walk, or sitting through faculty meetings, I could keep calling on our Lord Jesus. After four weeks of using the Jesus Prayer, I began to pray in tongues, like other members of the prayer group. Then, week by week, other charismatic gifts came: prophecy, speaking messages in tongues, interpreting tongues, and teaching the gospel.

Union with God. I learned a most important lesson in this period, namely, that Christianity is neither an ideal way of life nor a search for some exalted state of consciousness. It is personal union with the Triune God, in the Holy Spirit, through Christ, to the Father. This is the goal of life and the center of the faith. This interpersonal union with God necessarily requires union with his church, the body of Christ here on earth. If this were true, I could cease the yoga exercises and everything else that I was doing to attain a higher state of consciousness. What I learned on my retreat finally sank in after being in the prayer group for a while: Christianity is a set of relationships, not a state of consciousness.

There remained still another hurdle for me: astrology. Though my interest had dwindled, I continued casting horoscopes on occasion. When the high school held three days of mini-courses in the spring, I offered the students some classes in astrology. Gently, the Lord brought me to repentance of astrology through reading Christian books.

The Holy Spirit gave me a hunger to read everything possible about the history of Pentecostalism, the charismatic gifts of tongues, prophecy, interpretation, healing, and the fruit of the Holy Spirit—love, joy, peace, patience, kindness, generosity, faithfulness, gentleness, chastity (Gal 5:22). Also wanting to better understand and defend the Christian faith, I read a lot of C.S. Lewis. I began with his *Chronicles of Narnia*, which drew me to read *Mere Christianity*, *The Problem of Pain*, and other apologetic books by this great author. My heart would soar while reading this intelligent convert from atheism describe the utter logic of belief in the virgin birth, Christ's redeeming death, and his bodily resurrection. He made the testimony of the apostles, as found in the Scriptures, sound so plausible. Yet he used clear, simple examples to communicate deep truths. From reading his books, I learned to teach the Christian faith in my classes instead of weird meditations. The classes went much better, and I even came to enjoy teaching the students, once I tried teaching them the Catholic faith.

The Holy Spirit and You (by Dennis and Rita Bennett, a charismatic Episcopalian priest and his wife) was particularly instrumental in helping me repent of astrology. The Bennetts included a section about the "works of the flesh" listed in Galatians 5:19-20: immorality, idolatry, sorcery, hatred, rivalry, factions, drunkenness, orgies, and other sins. They identified sorcery as ouija boards, séances, Tarot cards, the *I Ching*, and astrology. It struck my conscience deeply. Anxiety about committing serious sin made me stop reading and reconsider my behavior.

I clung to a scientific basis for astrology, as taught by Jung, but the Bennetts showed how sacred Scripture condemned occult practices (Lv 19:26, 31; Dt 18:9-14; Is 47:9-15). Now I had to decide whether I would use Jung's permission to practice the occult or obey God. There was no real conflict in making my choice. I threw out all of my astrology books and *ephemerides* to be burnt. Feeling relieved and cleansed, I returned to my easy chair to continue reading *The Holy Spirit and You*.

After a few minutes, I wondered whether God had just been testing me to see if I was free enough to be rid of astrology paraphernalia. Perhaps I could fetch the books back to my room and resume my horoscopes in a more spiritual way. However, the overwhelming sense I felt was to let those books go into the incinerator and keep reading the Bennetts, C.S. Lewis, and other Christian writers. Never have I regretted that decision. Of course, as the seriousness of the sin of occultism dawned on me, I confessed it. That too was, as usual, a great relief and joy.

The very next week a team from the Ursuline prayer group invited me to help them teach a Life in the Spirit Seminar to introduce local parishioners to the release of the Holy Spirit in their lives. At the end of this seven-week seminar, Fr. Richard Rohr invited me to join the prayer group's leadership team, which was about to be named the "New Jerusalem" prayer group. This opened many doors for preaching, teaching Scripture, and giving talks and seminars about Christ. All this gave me greater joy than foolish occultism ever could. The Lord even used me to help some teenagers involved in the occult experience spiritual freedom from its influences through prayer and counseling. It was all a wonderful preparation for the priesthood, for which I am still grateful.

However, even as I was experiencing newfound freedom in Christ, New Age ideas and practices were infiltrating the church and seducing good Catholics with their siren song of spiritual power and enlightenment. The next chapter explores some of those beliefs and practices which have become increasingly popular in the 1990s.

SEVEN

Catholic Involvement in the New Age

A FTER A TWO-YEAR STINT of teaching at St. Xavier High, Fr. Provincial approved me for theology studies and ordination. The enneagram was not such a hot item at the seminary anymore. Hardly anyone remembered it by the time I returned. A few times I invited friends to look at it and identify their ego numbers. Fitting someone into one mold or another seemed like fun, especially if we shared the same compulsion and talked about it. However, after incorrectly typing some friends, I eventually dropped the enneagram from my repertoire of spiritual direction tools. Also it was too complex to explain repeatedly to people.

Studying Scripture was particularly exciting since the Word of God is so central in charismatic prayer groups. Reading Protestant books about the Pentecostal experience raised a lot of questions about the relationship between the Catholic faith and sacred Scripture. Is Catholicism rooted in Scripture? What is the biblical warrant for devotion to Mary and the saints? the Eucharist? confession? the papacy? These questions spurred me to study Scripture and the early Fathers of the Church.

An older, extremely intelligent professor, Fr. Edmund Fortman, S.J., offered a course called "Witchcraft, Demon-

ology, and Exorcism." Our examination of witchcraft and
Satan worship and the church's response to them kept alive
an interest in the occult. Now I wanted to know how to combat it. Students at the high school and prayer group had gotten involved in the occult and demonic activities. Most of
them had attempted suicide at least once. Fr. Fortman's
course gave solid information about helping them. Yet even
in that academic setting I had to pray for spiritual protection
before reading occult or satanic literature.

Our seminary belonged to an ecumenical consortium of
seminaries on Chicago's south side, making available over
four hundred courses to its members. Fr. James Heisig,
S.V.D., a professor at a nearby Catholic seminary, taught spirituality courses from a Jungian perspective. A brilliant lecturer
with a phenomenal grasp of his material, he held a doctorate
from Oxford and studied at the Carl Jung Institute in Zurich,
Switzerland. I took two of his courses and a seminar in Jung.
Perhaps Jung was wrong about the *I Ching,* astrology, and the
occult, but I thought certainly he had deep insight into
human psychology.

However, in the seminar, Heisig balanced any romance
about Jung with sober assessments. He warned us about two
qualities of Jungianism. First, Jung does not have the final
answers in the field of psychology. Freud and other psychologists have many genuine insights into the psyche, and Jung
needs to be balanced by them. Many psychologists have
since confirmed this insight. It seems that the majority of
psychologists do not depend on Jung's therapeutic insights
as much as religious people do.

Heisig's second warning was about Jung's theology.
Though Jung believed in deity, it was a polytheistic faith.
Jung believed in all the gods, wherever they came from.
Furthermore, Heisig warned that Jung's information about
myths was quite limited and superficial. He filtered out
information from other religions when it did not fit his theories, or he adapted the information to fit his theories. Most

people do the same, so do not single out Jung for being a fallible human. We should simply accept his theories and information with open eyes.

Having kept a lively interest in spirituality, I asked our director of studies for permission to get a masters degree when I finished the requirements for the seminary a little ahead of schedule. A degree in Scripture seemed out of the question since I doubted my ability for it. A degree in spirituality with a strong Scripture component seemed more realistic. A new program in Creation Centered Spirituality at Mundelein College in Chicago, founded by Dominican Fr. Matthew Fox, O.P., looked interesting. I hoped to join at the ground level.

Fr. Gannon, S.J., the director of studies, said no. He had serious misgivings about the academic quality of the program and its benefits. Furthermore, the provincial wanted me to teach at Loyola Academy, our high school in Wilmette, Illinois.

Not again! Not another high school! A couple years in Cincinnati was good for me, but not again! This time I had more faith that God wanted me at this assignment, but I still did not like it. I wanted nothing to do with teaching high school kids. Yet I believed in the importance of obedience to one's superiors.

Despite my strong emotional reaction, God had some important things for me to do and learn in Wilmette. Soon after arriving at Loyola Academy, a group of lay people interested in ministry to young people asked for help in starting a parish prayer group. I accepted and enjoyed the work. In my second year at Loyola Academy, a group of permanent deacons asked for a course in the Old Testament. Little did I realize how our Lord would use this opportunity to redirect my career. The course preparation was exciting, and the classes went extremely well. I was even asked to repeat the course. Based on this success and on my continued dislike of high school teaching, I asked Fr. Gannon if I could pursue doctoral studies in Old Testament at Vanderbilt University. Surprisingly, he was willing to take the risk. He let me study Hebrew and Greek for a year, take Old Testament courses, and apply to Vanderbilt (and elsewhere), and then see what would happen. The language courses were fun, Vanderbilt accepted me, so I moved to Nashville in 1979. This move launched me on my career as a Scripture scholar, studying and eventually teaching on the university level. This seemed like a move away from concerns about the occult, witchcraft, enneagrams, and related topics.

Life as a Jesuit has been wonderful. Doctoral studies in Old Testament, priestly ministry, and now teaching at Loyola University in Chicago have all contributed to a delightful life. I would never trade them away. Christ Jesus calls us priests to be shepherds of the flock, good shepherds like him. However, when thieves try to break into the sheepfold, Christ expects us to stand fast against them and confront them with Jesus, who is Truth incarnate. Through various circumstances I believe that the Lord has called me to warn the sheep about the wolves, some of whom wear sheep's clothing. This is how I began to research current trends in the New Age Movement.

FIRST INTRODUCTION TO CURRENT NEW AGE TRENDS

One morning early in the fall semester of 1987, a bright young student invited me to a lecture being offered in her dorm. Sr. Gabe Uhlein, O.S.F., would lead a "conversation" on "Planetary consciousness: the earth as a paradigm for spirituality." Sr. Gabe is an associate of Fr. Matthew Fox, O.P., who "translated" St. Hildegard of Bingen's works for him. This very bright woman spoke about changing paradigms, that is, the key concepts for understanding the world. She insisted that since we all come from the earth, she is our mother. Further, the sun is our grandmother and the universe is our great-grandmother.

Uhlein told us that a real consciousness permeates the material world, as seen in the story of the "Hundredth Monkey." She reported that a Macaque monkey on Koshima Island near Japan learned to wash sweet potatoes before eating them. Soon other monkeys on the island learned it. Then monkeys on other islands began to wash their sweet potatoes. Lyall Watson's book, *Lifetide*, claimed that when the number of potato-washing monkeys reached about one hundred, the troop had attained a critical mass of consciousness about washing that reached monkeys throughout the islands.

For Sr. Uhlein and for New Agers, this became a paradigm of new human consciousness. Once a critical mass of people rethink their attitude toward the earth, peace, harmony, and justice, everyone will suddenly change their way of thinking. The change depended on only an elite few leading the way. She and her Franciscan Sisters belonged to the 10 percent of the world changing their paradigm. Soon everyone else would follow. She invited the audience to join this inevitable, unstoppable paradigm shift in thought and culture.

Unfortunately, Sr. Uhlein did not tell us the rest of the story. Dr. Ron Amundson researched the hundredth monkey and learned that the story was bogus. The scholars who did the original research on the islands were not perplexed by the phenomenon of monkeys washing potatoes on other islands. Rather, Amundson learned that one monkey, Jugo, swam to another island and stayed there for four years. When confronted with this and other scientific facts, Watson admitted that the story of the hundredth monkey was a "metaphor" for consciousness raising based on "hearsay." This is a good example of the type of malarkey foisted upon the public by some advocates of consciousness raising.

Sr. Gabe's mixture of gnosticism, pantheism, and pseudoscience was perplexing. Bothersome, too, was another nun's advice that students meditate on crystals to tap into their metaphysical powers. She told one of my students a tale about the enormous crystal on the lost continent of Atlantis that powered all vehicles in the air, on land, sea, and under the sea. Intrigued, he wanted to learn more about this non-polluting power. Concerned by all this, I began researching the New Age Movement. The introduction of this book summarizes my research in the New Age Movement, but other aspects of it need further explanation, especially as they pertain to NAM's inroads into Catholicism.

The end result is the following apologetic.

WHAT'S THE BIG DEAL ABOUT CRYSTALS?

The story of crystal power in Atlantis is a common New Age myth. Edgar Cayce, the "sleeping prophet," and Ruth Montgomery, his posthumous disciple, both write about crystal power in Atlantis. Books, conventions, and stores specialize in crystal power. Why? Because crystals are key to the coming New Age, according to Katrina Raphaell and other experts in the field.

Monism, the belief that all is one, and popularized notions about science, underlie crystal mysticism. Modern physics tells us that all subatomic structures are composed of light. Since light travels in waves, it is a vibration. Therefore, the real oneness of the universe is the cosmic force of light moving at various vibrations. Human beings are composed of light vibrations, not only physically but spiritually and mentally. Since crystal molecules pulsate at the same frequency, they align harmoniously with the essence of the universe. Therefore, crystals help humans transcend their minds and align with the one essence. This is all claimed in addition to their usefulness in watches, computers, and lasers.

Katrina Raphaell identifies two ways crystals affect the mind. First, like a mirror, they "reflect light into the consciousness" and thereby "reflect your own wisdom back to you."[1] Apparently they are a tool for meditation to draw out ideas already in the mind. Second, crystals have their own consciousness, so they can teach and befriend humans. One can listen carefully "to their silent voice" and learn their secrets. Then they respond, which helps them to "evolve and fulfill their higher destiny."

The crystals taught Raphaell the ideas in her book.[2] Harley Swiftdeer, a shaman/psychologist, identified crystals as the "brain cells and memory of Mother Earth." They can bring humans into alignment and increase one's memory capacity. However, each individual must do this on his or her own, which prohibits worship of Jesus, according to Swiftdeer. "Jesus said, 'Even as I am you also shall be and even greater works shall you do.' You can't do greater works than someone if you put them above you and give your power away to it."[3]

New Agers believe that crystals are essential to the coming new Age of Aquarius. Raphaell believes that humans have only two choices before them: either let go of "past outdated systems, programming, concepts, and ideologies" so as to embrace the "laws of love" and life; or die and destroy the whole human race. She believes that right now certain "New Age stones" and the knowledge to use them have emerged to help people enter the Age of Aquarius. People should "join forces with these stones" to create this new age, new world, and new humanity.[4] Others claim that dolphins are bringing up crystals from Atlantis to help transform the New Age. Still others simply go to Seaworld to talk to the dolphins directly.

The crystals are not neutral stones for New Agers and Christians. An audience applauded Swiftdeer's challenge to stop worshiping Jesus and become like him. If angels must worship Jesus (Heb 1:6 "Let all the angels of God worship him"), so must we humans. Rather, let stones and crystals give glory to God by being stones! Crystals vibrate when electricity is applied to them, and they generate piezoelectric energy when squeezed and let go—not otherwise. They are beautiful and so Revelation 21:18-21 describes the crystal decorations of the new and heavenly Jerusalem. Crystals are useful for clocks, computers, radios, and lasers. They give glory to God in ways that are proper to them as crystals.

However, we should not promote a myth about their vibrational help in consciousness raising. Crystals vibrate at millions of cycles per second, while human brain waves oscillate at about two hundred cycles per second. Nor is it sensible to mythologize our silicon kinship with crystals, because the silicon dioxide in quartz has only three atoms per molecule, while the extremely complex silicon in the human body has fifty thousand atoms per molecule.[5] Simplification and misinformation can make us sound like we have rocks in our heads, which does not glorify God. St. Paul's speech on Mars Hill, Athens, is instructive: "Being offspring of God, therefore, we ought not to think the divine nature to be like gold or silver or stone, an engraved work of art and of human imagination" (Acts 17:29).

We are God's creations by nature and his children by adoption, created to worship God only. Let the creatures be creatures and God be the sole divinity. We will love creatures far more by accepting their creaturely limits than by divinizing them. Once we attribute divine power to creatures, they can only disappoint us. Their limitations show they are not worthy to be God. Accepting them as fellow creatures means accepting their natural limitations and loving them as such. So must it be with crystals, people, and every other wonderful creation of God.

SPIRITISM REINCARNATED AS CHANNELING

Halloween news flash: Ruth Berger, a Tupperware saleswoman, discovered her powers as a medium while reading a handwriting analysis booklet in the supermarket check-out line. Now she is scheduled to address an ecumenical group of widows at St. Peter's Catholic Church library in Skokie,

Illinois. These elderly and presumably conservative Catholics and Protestants meditated for a while and waited for the spirits to speak.[6]

The tradition of mediumship and channeling is as American as Ichabod Crane or Mark Twain's "Golden Arm" story. In 1849 two teenagers, the Fox sisters, heard a table in their home "rap" sharply. They interpreted it as a message, perhaps from a man who had been murdered in the house, and continued the practice of conjuring spirits until their deaths. Pilgrimages to their home in upstate New York started a fad of spiritism. Many persons made a living by communicating with the dead for the living. Others, like Harry Houdini, occupied themselves with exposing the mediums' trickery. Still others organized spiritist churches and denominations, combining hymn singing, sermons, and séances. Some of the old-style mediums and spiritist churches are still around, but New Agers prefer "channeling."

Instead of a spirit form or voice heard by a small group holding hands around a rising table, channelers allow themselves to be taken over by one or more spirits. Their voices and facial expressions might change when the spirit of Seth (Jane Roberts), Ramtha (J.Z. Knight), Lazaris (Jack Purcell), or others takes control. Channelers usually go into a trance-like sleep, close their eyes, and let their chins drop to their chests. Then their eyes open, their heads come up, and another voice speaks through them. Fake British accents are popular, probably because they sound intelligent and sophisticated to Americans.

There are a variety of problems with channeling. Common sense says that handing over control of one's personality to someone other than yourself or God is dangerous. If common sense does not stop one, then know that sacred Scripture explicitly forbids it: "Do not turn to mediums or familiar spirits; do not seek to be defiled by them; I am Yahweh your God" (Lv 19:31). "As for the person who turns to mediums and familiar spirits to go after them: I will set my face against that person and cut him off from among the people" (Lv 20:6). "And when they say to you, 'Should not a people seek its gods, [go] to the dead for the sake of the living, for instruction and for a testimony?' Certainly they will speak according to this word, which has no light" (Is 8:19-20). This last passage means people prefer mediums and channelers to seeking God in "instruction" (Hebrew, *Torah*), which refers to the Scriptures.

One reason God forbids mediumship and channeling is that the spirits never tell the truth about God. The spirits may reveal a few secret tidbits from someone's life, and these things may be true, even if inconsequential. However, the spirits do not have a great track record on foretelling the future. For instance, Cayce was way off on predictions about Atlantis rising above sea level. Walter Martin calculated Jeanne Dixon's record for correct predictions at about 27 percent.

A still more decisive aspect of God's prohibition of channeling is that the spirits are absolutely consistent in teaching falsehoods about Jesus Christ and God. For instance, "Seth" is a spirit supposedly encountered by a young Catholic woman in New York during the 1960s. She and her husband were "playing" with a Ouija board, and the spirit "Seth" took over. Eventually, he got bored with the Ouija board and took control of Jane. Her husband wrote down the messages for what became the first commercially successful channeling book (Russell Chandler says it proves one can "perish and still publish"). Seth's gospel about Christ is bizarre:

> Seth says that Christ did not exist as one historic person. "There were three men whose lives became confused in history and merged, and whose composite history became known as the life of Christ.... Each was highly gifted psychically, knew of his role, and accepted it willingly. The three men were part of one entity, gaining physical existence in one time. The entity was born once

as John the Baptist, and then he was born in two other forms. One of these contained the personality that most stories of Christ refer to.... The race called up these personalities from its own psychic bank, from the pool of individualized consciousness that was available to it."[7]

"I [Seth] mentioned the Crucifixion, saying once that it was an actuality and a reality, although it did not take place in your [physical] time. It took place in the same sort of time in which a dream occurs and its reality was felt by generations. Not being a physical reality, it influenced the world of physical matter in a way that no purely physical event could. Seth is *not* saying that the Crucifixion was "just a dream." He is saying that though it did not occur *historically*, it did happen within another reality and emerged into history as an *idea* rather than a physical event—an idea that changed civilization. [According to Seth, of course, an idea *is* an event, whether physically materialized or not.] Seth goes on to say: "The Ascension [of Christ] did not occur in time as you know it. It is also a contribution of the universe of dreams to your physical system."[8]

Ruth Montgomery, sometimes called the "First Lady of the New Age Movement," contacts Lilly. She also contacts the famous "pope of spiritism" Arthur Ford, her own father, along with other spirits through automatic writing. Actually, she types since it is faster. Through her the spirits teach about Christ's reincarnations and consciousness, despite the complete absence of any of this material in the New Testament record. She and Edgar Cayce wrote that Jesus is a reincarnation of Amelius, who has been Adam and Eve and about one hundred other people.[9] Her spirits' explanation of the resurrection depends more on extra-terrestrials than on God: "By manipulating atoms they could appear and disappear at will.... It was a demonstration to earthlings of what they could again achieve if they too divorced themselves from the physical magnet of earth and became as thought forms, lighter than air. Intricate drawings of these atomic disassemblers were left behind in various places, drawn not by the humans who saw them but by these so-called gods from outer space.... It is the way Jesus left the tomb without trace of his body."[10] These spirits also misrepresent Christ's Second Coming:

> ... later in the twenty-first century Jesus is planning to return to earth in a supreme try to restore God's kingdom here.... The Master will come again as a babe, to Mary.[11]

> "The Christ spirit will enter a perfected person within some twenty to thirty years after the earth has restabilized," the Guides continued, recalling the merging of the Divine Christ spirit with the man called Jesus, at the time of His baptism.[12]

First, notice the contradiction in the spirits' doctrine. The "Christ spirit" will enter some perfected person after a catastrophe initiates the New Age, yet Jesus will come again to Mary as a baby. Jesus our Lord and his apostles spoke frequently about his Second Coming, but they never promised anything like Montgomery's teaching. Jesus claims that everyone in the world will "see the Son of Man coming on the clouds of heaven with power and great glory" (Mt 24:30; 25:31); he will not be reborn as a baby. The incarnation, like his death and resurrection, took place within the real world of time and space (not Seth's dream world), once and for all.

Second, Montgomery's spirits contradict Scripture and the church about Christ's nature. Catholic teaching follows the Gospels of Luke and Matthew in claiming that Jesus is God the Son conceived in the womb of Mary. "The angel said to her, 'The Holy Spirit shall come upon you and the power of the Most High will overshadow you, therefore the holy one being born of you will be called Son of God'" (Lk 1:35; see also Mt 1:20-23). God the Word, the Second Person of the Blessed Trinity, became flesh (Jn 1:14). That is why the Catholic church calls Mary the Mother of God because Jesus is truly God. He did not become God at his baptism in the Jordan. Rather, the Father manifested Jesus' divinity by saying, "This is my beloved Son in whom I am well pleased," (Mt 3:17; Mk 1:11; Lk 3:22) and the Holy Spirit appeared as a dove hovering over him. One must choose between believing Ruth Montgomery or Matthew, Mark, Luke, and John.

Another popular and financially successful channeler is the Yelms, Washington, housewife J.Z. Knight, through whom Ramtha supposedly speaks. Ramtha is reputed to be a thirty-five-thousand-year-old warrior king from Atlantis, whose British accent has to do since no one knows how an Atlantis accent sounds. Like most New Agers and channelers, she claims everyone is the Christ and God. This power is so great that if Ramtha cut off your arm, you would have the power to grow another one back. She says the lord god of your being is the soul. It weighs thirteen ounces and is in harmony with all that is. "Who answers your prayers? *You* do! Know who you are and embrace that divinity. There is no one grander than you. Only those who understand truth, the simplicity that you are God, that Christ is within you, will enter the profound age."[13] Knight says Ramtha "loves all people and all things," but some people have to go through "the church syndrome or guru syndrome." Eventually these will fail, leaving them here alone. One day they will realize, "you're really it; there's no one else but you. That's why the entity says it's you, *you, you!*"[14]

The teaching that everyone is God and Christ typifies New Age doctrine, but not New Testament teaching. Rather, Jesus and St. Paul warn us frequently that "other christs," "other gospels," and "other spirits" may deceive anyone oblivious to the possibility of falsehood.

But I fear lest, as the serpent deceived Eve by his trickery, your thoughts may be seduced from the simplicity and purity which is in Christ. For if indeed one comes preaching another Jesus which we did not preach, or you accept another spirit which you did not receive, or you put up with another gospel which you did not receive, you submit to it readily enough. (2 Cor 11:3-4)

I marvel that so quickly you are moving away from the one who called you by the grace of Christ to another gospel, not that there is another. Only there are those who trouble you and wish to pervert the gospel of Christ. But even if we or an angel from heaven should evangelize you with a gospel besides what we preached to you, let him be a curse. As we have previously said, I say now again, if anyone evangelizes you with a gospel besides what you have received, let him be accursed. (Gal 1:6-9)

Now the Spirit definitely says that in the last times some will turn away from the faith, going to deceiving spirits and the teachings of demons, of men who speak lies in hypocrisy. (1 Tm 4:1-2)

Then if anyone says to you, "Behold, here is the Christ!" or, "Here!" do not believe. For false christs and false prophets will arise, and they will give great signs and wonders so as to deceive, if it were possible, even the elect. Behold, I say it to you beforehand. Therefore, if they say to you, "Behold, he is in the desert!" do not go out; "Behold, he is in the private rooms!" do not believe. For just as the lightening goes out from the east and is seen in the west, so will be the presence of the Son of Man. (Mt 24:23-27)

There is only one Christ, Jesus the Lord. He proved his messiahship and divinity by rising from the dead. The spirits and their channelers have given no such proof. Instead, they contradict the clear teaching of Scripture and the church in order to "tickle ears." Jesus says in Revelation 22:13-15: "I am the Alpha and the Omega, the First and the Last, the Beginning and the End. Happy are those who wash their garments so that they may have authority over the tree of life and may enter the city by the gates. Outside are the dogs and the sorcerers, and the fornicators and the murderers and the idolaters and everyone who loves and does falsehood." May we always be blessed, never loving or doing falsehood.

This text in Revelation teaches another point which the spirits and most New Agers reject: divinely given morality. Typical of the New Age Movement is Ramtha's (J.Z. Knight) doctrine, "There is no right or wrong, there simply is, so you don't have to accept anybody's truth. You can create your own truth, whatever is plausible and true for you."[15]

Many others hold the same amorality. The late Sri Rajneesh said, "My ashram makes no difference between the demonic and the divine."[16] According to Swami Vivekananda, "Good and evil are one and the same"; "the Murderer, too, is God."[17] "Emmanuel," channeled by Pat Rodegast, says that Hitler and Stalin should not be condemned too severely because they are also part of God.[18] Marilyn Ferguson's influential New Age book, *Aquarian Conspiracy*, concurs on the absence of real moral norms: "Human nature is neither good nor bad but open to continuous transformation and transcendence. It only has to discover itself...."[19] "In these spiritual traditions [from the Orient] there is neither good nor evil. There is only light and the absence of light... wholeness and brokenness... flow and struggle."[20] And Shirley MacLaine is in complete agreement: "There is no such thing as evil. Evil is fear and uncertainty. Evil is what you *think* it is."[21]

This widespread amoral belief makes New Age doctrine very attractive. While claiming to be very spiritual, you do not have to keep any moral principle except by personal preference. After all, if you are God, you can create your own commandments, ten, more, or less. Leonard Orr did by devising ten commandments for the New Age. For example.

"Thou shalt not have any other gods before me," means Orr and his readers should worship themselves alone since everyone is innately divine. "Thou shalt not commit adultery" means not adulterating or watering down one's own divinity. Each divine person can declare himself or herself to be married to whomever they choose whenever they choose, even if it is multiple persons in a single day.[22]

Three women told me about concrete examples of the channelers' New Age immorality. After their husbands consulted channelers, the spirits told two of them that in the seventeenth century they had been married to other women, whom they had abandoned. To make up for the bad karma this caused, they abandoned their present wives to remarry the wives of former lifetimes. The third husband was told that his present wife had been his daughter in a previous life, so he ended marital relations and abandoned her and his children.

These ideas completely contradict the moral and just requirements of the Lord God in both the Old and New Testaments. "Be holy because I, the Lord your God, am holy" (Lv 19:2; 1 Pt 1:16) and "Be perfect as your heavenly Father is perfect" (Mt 5:48) are commands addressed to us. The Ten Commandments are not a multiple-choice selection, but a set of requirements for anyone who enters into the covenant relationship of God's committed love for us. These holy commands define how we are to live for God. Once a rich young man asked Jesus, "Good Teacher, what must I do to inherit everlasting life?" Jesus' answer was to obey the commandments, give up all else, and come and follow him (Mk 10:17-19).

NEW AGE CULT FOR CATHOLICS

A New Age cult has been particularly successful in converting Catholics—the Church Universal and Triumphant.

This group comes from the theosophy tradition of occultism begun by Madame Helena Petrovna Blavatsky.[23] After visiting the Fox sisters in 1875, Blavatsky, with the help of disciples Colonel Henry S. Olcott and William Q. Judge, started the Theosophical Society in New York. Blavatsky claimed to have contacted the Ascended Masters of the Great White Brotherhood, a council of developed souls who promised to incarnate soon and govern the human race. Blavatsky returned to Adyar, India, in 1879 to start an *ashram* (monastery). There the Ascended Masters would supposedly be better able to communicate their messages written in liquid light for Blavatsky to read. By 1888, Blavatsky was in London to found the Esoteric School of Theosophy, where she died in 1891.

Many groups splintered off from theosophy in subsequent years. Some theosophy splinter groups with their own revelations from the Ascended Masters include the tradition founded by Baird T. Spalding. He claims to have traveled to the Orient in 1894, where he learned of the Ascended Masters. In the 1920s, he wrote books about the Masters, who had taught him the concept of the divine consciousness within all human beings called the great "I AM."

Guy and Edna Ballard had been studying Blavatsky and Spalding when Guy claims to have met Count St. Germain, an Ascended Master purportedly in charge of the present Seventh Golden Age, on Mount Shasta in California. Ballard published the messages from Ascended Master St. Germain about the presence of "I AM," the individualized God presence in every human being. He taught that at the center of the universe is the Great Central Sun, from which individualized presences of God come forth as great "I AM" human beings. In this theology, "Christ" is an impersonal force which every enlightened person can eventually realize. The key is allowing St. Germain's "Violet Consuming Flame" to purify all sins and negative influences.[24]

As with other Theosophical leaders, the Ballards believed that they were the only messengers for the Ascended Masters.

Anyone else who received messages was excommunicated from the "I AM" movement. However, Guy Ballard died in 1939 and Edna's messages became ever less frequent. Others began to hear from the Ascended Masters, extraterrestrials, or both. They started still other organizations.

Perhaps the most eminent successors of the Ballards have been Mark and Elizabeth Clare Prophet, founders of the Summit Lighthouse and the Church Universal and Triumphant (CUT). Though Mark died in 1973, he supposedly continues to coauthor many books and channel with his wife, Elizabeth Clare, or "Guru Ma" as she is now called by her *chelas* (disciples).

She contacts a wide assortment of Ascended Masters, including El Morya, the Chief of the Darjeeling (India) Council of the Great White Brotherhood and founder of The Summit Lighthouse, Lord of the First Ray, incarnated as Melchior the Magi, King Arthur, Thomas à Becket, and Thomas More. Akbar the Great Mogul was Mark Prophet's master. Jesus is the Piscean Master who personified the Christ in the last age. St. Germain is the Aquarian Master who revealed the God consciousness of the "I AM" and continues to channel through Elizabeth Clare Prophet.

Others include the Ascended Lady Master, Mother Mary, who comes from the angelic kingdom and was chosen by the Father-Mother God to give birth to the Christ; Gautama Buddha, the Lord of the World, Great Teacher of Enlightenment, and Sponsor of Summit University; Kuthumi, the Lord of the Second Ray, formerly incarnate as Pythagoras, Balthasar the Magi, and Francis of Assisi, who now serves with Jesus as the World Teacher (he helped found the Theosophical Society by channeling through Blavatsky); the Ascended Lady Master Kuan Yin, the goddess and mediatrix of mercy and a member of the Karmic Board; Master Lanello, formerly Mark the Evangelist and, until 1973, Mark Prophet.[25] These Masters continue to teach, give orders, promise their destined incarnations for the New Age, and even foretell World War III. March of 1990 was the date they last set for World War III, but CUT's diligence during the crisis so pleased the Ascended Masters that they postponed the war.

CUT seems to attract many Catholics, as well as others, to its rolls. It offers a complex view of God, human beings and their purpose in life, and a conservative political agenda for the 1990s and beyond.

New Age Rosary. CUT's appeal to Catholics can be explained in part through their distorted devotion to Mary as an Ascended Master, especially in her apparitions as Our Lady of Fatima. Other apparitions are valid as well, but CUT devotees prefer connecting Fatima to their own belief in World War III. Since Mary is so important, they say a type of Rosary, but it is hardly Catholic. The Sign of the Cross is made by saying, "In the name of the Father, the Mother, the Son, and the Holy Spirit."

In place of the Apostles' Creed, which belongs to Christianity of the Piscean Age, the first prayer is the universal creed of the "Keeper's Daily Prayer." It is a New Age prayer to center one's consciousness on the flame of God by claiming to be a "God Flame of radiant love, charged now with beloved Helios and Vesta's Supreme God Consciousness and Solar Awareness." This prayer is supposed to be superior to any "man-made doctrine or timeworn dogma," such as the Apostles' Creed.

The Lord's Prayer has also been rewritten for the New Age, as revealed by the "Galilean Master" to Mark Prophet on April 14, 1963:

Our Father who art in heaven, hallowed be Thy name, I AM. I AM Thy kingdom come, I AM Thy will being done on earth as it is in heaven. I AM giving this day daily bread to all. I AM forgiving all life this day even as I AM all life forgiving me. I AM leading all men away from temptation,

I AM leading all men away from every evil condition. I AM the kingdom, I AM the power, and I AM the glory of God in eternal immortal manifestation. All this I AM.

Mark and Elizabeth Clare Prophet claim that Mother Mary asked the Mother of the Flame to change the "Hail Mary," too: "Hail, Mary, full of grace, the Lord is with thee. Blessed art thou amongst women and blessed is the fruit of thy womb, Jesus. Holy Mary, Mother of God, pray for us sons and daughters of God, now and at the hour of our victory over sin, disease and death." The "Glory Be" remains unaltered, except that at the end are added the words, "I AM, I AM, I AM." This New Age "Scriptural Rosary" is meant to bring enlightenment to all who pray it.[26]

Praying the Rosary is a tremendous form of devotion. In it we meditate on the key mysteries of our salvation as manifested in the life of Christ and his mother. CUT's Rosary, however, would lead its users astray to a New Age spirituality at odds with biblical Christianity.

CUT's Doctrine of God. CUT's doctrine of God can appear palatable to the unwary Christian as well. Elizabeth Clare Prophet insists that "monotheism remains the foundation of cosmic law." "God is still one—one individed [sic] Whole." Furthermore, God is a Trinity.[27] While these statements sound Christian enough, their context shows that CUT has a totally different understanding of God than the Catholic church.

For instance, another "cardinal principle of Ascended Master law" is that God dwells in every human being, not just Jesus Christ. Everyone has the "Christ-identity" coming from the "infinite Spirit of the Father-Mother God." The Ascended Master from Assisi says, "There is no difference between the Divine Nature in Jesus and the Divine Nature" in everyone else. The reason is that every individual is a spark from the "Central Sun," the principal energy source at the center of the cosmos. Each spark is "an exact replica of the original unity that was and is God," so each fragment within each person is "the very Presence of God Himself," known as the "I AM Presence."[28]

This doctrine is a classic statement of New Age monism and is incompatible with the Christian teaching that God alone is uncreated and that we humans are created in his image and likeness. On Mount Sinai, God gave his name to Moses: "I AM WHO AM." That name belongs to God alone. The appropriation of it by humans constitutes blasphemy from a traditional Catholic and Christian point of view.

CUT's doctrine of the Trinity is also contrary to Catholic belief, mostly because it depends not on Scripture and Church teaching but on doctrines revealed by the Ascended Masters of the Great White Brotherhood. The Trinity, for CUT, is merely the Western name for the same concept in Hinduism, where Brahma (the creator), Vishnu (the preserver), and Shiva (the destroyer and deliverer) form a trinity. Further, the first person of the trinity is the Alpha and the Omega, which stand for the Father and Mother, respectively.[29] The "Universal Mother" was "born out of the unity of the Divine Triad" as the "antithesis" of the Trinity. Because of this, humans can embody the synthesis of "Fourfold Attributes, Father, Son, Holy Spirit, and Mother."[30] Ascended Master St. Germain finds support for the presence of the feminine principle in the female counterparts to the Hindu triad: Brahma's consort is Sarasvati; Vishnu's is Lakshmi; and Shiva's is Parvati or Kali.[31]

Catholics and other Christians find these depictions of God a distortion of the doctrine of the Trinity. Further, Hindus do not regard Brahma, Vishnu, and Shiva as a trinity but as a triad, the top three gods in a pantheon of millions.

It is important here to state clearly what it is we believe as Catholics to avoid confusion. The Catholic doctrine of the Trinity holds the truths of both Old and New Testaments that the Lord our God is one; no other god existed before him, nor will any come into being after him. Yet this one God has Three Persons, co-equal in being and deserving of all worship, yet distinct in personal identity. While CUT's doctrine of God looks attractive, especially with its promise that CUT adepts will become christs and realize their "I AM Presence," it is not true to sacred Scripture and church teaching.

CUT may choose to regard traditional Catholic teaching as worn-out and stultified, but we proclaim that it is the doctrine handed on to us by the real Jesus Christ. No matter what the Ascended Masters Jesus, Mary, St. Germain, Morya, or Lanello say, we find our life and joy in the teachings of Jesus Christ and the church he established on the Rock of Peter and the other apostles. We would do well to hear again St. Paul's words: "I wonder that you are moving so quickly from the one who has called you by the grace of Christ to another gospel, which is not another, only some are troubling you and wishing to pervert the gospel of Christ. But even if we or an angel from heaven should preach another gospel except what we preached to you, let him be a curse" (Gal 1:6-8).

Bob is an example of a Catholic who became involved in the Church Universal and Triumphant. Bob, (not his real name) a scientist and Ph.D. who has done post-doctoral work, joined CUT at his aunt's urging.

Bob's first attraction resulted from the claims of his Aunt Maureen who claimed to have been healed by the controversial "Doctor" Milan Brych in the Cook Islands near Australia. When Dr. Brych moved to California and got into malpractice trouble, Aunt Maureen came to his defense. Elizabeth Clare Prophet, whose headquarters were then in nearby Malibu, California, became a willing ally in Brych's fight against the medical establishment, big government, and big business. Brych lost his case, so Aunt Maureen returned home to Australia. In 1985, "Guru Ma" (Elizabeth Clare Prophet) visited Australia on a "stump," a lecture tour to "cut free the light bearers" (get new members). She "cut free" Aunt Maureen and her daughter Melissa, who became members of CUT.

They tried to convince Bob to join CUT as well and taught him their Rosary. The claims of healing, his family's arguments, and Bob's reluctance to change his moral life and return to the sacraments led him to CUT.

"Guru Ma" announced that the astrological projections of the Ascended Masters of the Great White Brotherhood indicated World War III would begin in March of 1990. Bob flew to CUT's Wyoming bomb shelters near Yellowstone National Park where he helped coordinate the "War Alert Office," awaiting news of the coming war. March passed. April passed. There were no signs of World War III.

Finally, Bob took a science job in another city. A co-worker told him about the beautiful Catholic cathedral in town, a "must-see" for visitors. As he walked in, an altar to the Blessed Virgin Mary attracted his attention. Suddenly, he knew he belonged. He had come home.

He returned to the Catholic faith and let go of CUT's spirituality, end-of-the-world predictions, and New Age Rosary. He confessed his sins, attended Mass, and even made a pilgrimage to a Marian shrine in Europe. He feels like he just woke up from sleep walking, typical for many people whose New Age involvement has had cultic tones to it.

But what are we to make of Fr. Matthew Fox, O.P.? He doesn't claim to be a New Ager, but many of his teachings on Creation Centered Spirituality have a New Age ring to them. And his spirituality is very attractive to many Catholics. Exploring his spirituality is the subject of our next chapter.

EIGHT

Matthew Fox and Creation Centered Spirituality

A S STATED EARLIER, my first stimulus to research current trends in the New Age Movement came after a talk on campus by Sr. Gabrielle Uhlein. Sr. Gabrielle "translated" the writings of St. Hildegard of Bingen, a medieval abbess and mystic, for Bear & Company. The genius behind Bear Press and the Institute for Creation Centered Spirituality, is Fr. Matthew Fox, O.P. This talented man directs the institute at the College of the Holy Names in California. He also teaches, writes prolifically, and lectures around the world. His faculty at the institute includes the witch Starhawk—a scholar and feminist author in the Wicca (witchcraft) tradition—a physicist and cosmologist Brian Swimme, a shaman, and others.

Is Matthew Fox a New Ager? Does he promote the movment? Where does he stand on Catholic faith? The problems with his writing fit into three categories: the quality of his scholarship, his worldview, and his theology.

FOX'S SCHOLARSHIP

Fr. Matthew Fox, O.P., did his doctoral work under M.D. Chenu, but was not influenced enough by that scholar. Fox's extensive interests and background include late Neoplatonist philosophy, medieval spirituality, and ecology. However, his scholarship is sloppy and embarrassing. Nonspecialists trust scholars to do their homework. Betraying that trust, as Fox sometimes does, casts a dark shadow on all scholars.

Questionable Scripture Scholarship. I first noticed problems with Fox's use of Scripture, which is my area of expertise. He mistranslates texts or misrepresents linguistic findings. For instance, he writes: "The word for 'mountain' in Hebrew also means 'the Almighty' and it comes from the word for breast. Mountains are the breasts of Mother Earth, thus 'Come! Play on my mountain of myrrh.'"[1] This is a rather confused batch of misinformation. "Mountain" in Hebrew is *har.* The name, "God Almighty," comes from the Akkadian word, *El Shaddai.* "Breast" in Hebrew is *shad,* from the root *shadah,* which is not the root of *Shaddai; shadad* is. While it is a small point, Fox mixes and matches etymologies irresponsibly to make a feminist point that does not exist in the ancient languages.

Another example occurs in his comments on the Song of Songs:

[The male lover in Song of Solomon] invokes the earth goddesses in this charge; this man is not out of touch with the prepatriarchal spirituality:

I tell you, O young ones of the holy city:
Do not arouse my lover before her time.
I charge you by the "spirits and the goddesses of the field,"
by the gazelles and the hinds: Do not disturb
my love while she is at rest (2:7).[2]

Fox's translation and comments are faulty. The Hebrew reads: "I adjure you, O daughters of Jerusalem:/by the gazelles or by the hinds of the field:/Do not awaken, do not stir not up love until she pleases" (2:7). The Hebrew word "gazelles" is *sebaoth*, similar to "hosts" in the name "Lord Sabaoth." The Greek Septuagint translates this as "by the powers and forces of the field." The Aramaic Targum has "by the Lord of Hosts and by the strength of the land of Israel." One scholar Jouon considered it an allusion to the armies of angels and their leaders, but the majority of modern scholars see these as words for gazelles and deer.[3] It does not refer to earth goddesses.

Fox abuses etymology when he claims that "the Hebrew word for blessing, *berakah*, is closely related to the word for create, *bara*.... The word for covenant, *beriyth*, is also directly related to the words for 'create' and for 'blessing.'"[4] In fact, no etymological connection exists among these Hebrew words. Covenants and creation may be blessings, but Fox derives his point from an error. Why does he do this? Is he trying to impress readers with scholarly authority to make other claims beyond his expertise?

In another place, Fox makes a significantly erroneous claim about the Hebrew language to support an equally erroneous statement about God. "The with-ness of God is especially significant because, while Greeks focus on nouns in their literature, Jews focus on prepositions such as with, against, from, etc. The covenant is a sign of God's with-ness. To be without covenant would be unbearable for the Jewish believer. God, then, is a preposition for the Jew. And the preposition is basically one of presence, of with-ness."[5] In fact, the Hebrew language does not focus on prepositions but on verbs, usually in the form of triliteral roots. The prepositions are substantives *derived from verbs*. The words meaning "God" are not prepositions, nor are they derived from prepositions.

Fox even retranslates a New Testament word that is not even in the New Testament! He writes of "the counsel of

Jesus to his friends" (substituting the word "culture" for *keno-sis*) when he declared that they be "in the culture but not of it."[6] First, the Greek word *kenosis* does not appear anywhere in the New Testament. Given that fact, why does Fox bother to retranslate it? Second, the saying of Jesus, which he re-interprets here, is apparently John 17:16, "They [the disciples] are not of the world [*ek tou kosmou*] as I am not of the world [*ek tou kosmou*]." Perhaps Fox did not want to inform his readers that neither Jesus nor his friends were "of the cosmos," since the cosmos is so important to Fox's theology of the "Cosmic Christ."

Serious problems arise with Fox's translation of the Gospel of John 1:1-5, 9, 10, 12, 14, where he uses "Creative Energy" to translate the Greek word *logos* (usually translated as "word"). Why not use "creative speaking" for *logos* and *dabhar* (Greek and Hebrew for "word") instead of "energy"? Further, for the personal pronoun "he" (present in Greek), Fox uses "it" to refer to the Word eleven times, though he calls "it" the "Child of the Creator." This depersonalizes the Word made flesh and transforms Christ into an impersonal energy. Further evidence of a depersonalizing tendency appears in this Mechtild of Magdeburg quote: "From the very beginning God loved us. The Holy Trinity gave *itself* in the creation of all things and made us, body and soul, in infinite love[7] (emphasis added).

Another type of misrepresentation appears in Fox's exe-gesis. He complains that Christians have allegorized the Song of Songs, "reading into the Jewish tradition a dualism between body and soul and an alien original sin mentality that are not there."[8] However, it was the rabbinic tradition that first allegorized the Song of Songs. Had Rabbi Aqiba not insisted on an allegorical interpretation of the Song, the rabbis would not have kept it in their Scripture canon at the Council of Yavneh (ca. A.D. 100). Christians simply contin-ued the Jewish tradition of allegorizing the song, though they adapted it to their faith in Christ.

Training in Hebrew helped me catch these errors, but I am not an expert in medieval literature. I asked other scholars about Fox's work. They criticized its defective and allegedly deceptive qualities.

Fox and Medieval Scholarship. Dr. Barbara Newman, an expert on St. Hildegard of Bingen at Northwestern University, is skeptical of Fox's work on St. Hildegard. In a footnote, she says of Gabrielle Uhlein's *Meditations with Hildegard of Bingen* and Fox's *Illuminations of Hildegard of Bingen*, that the "so-called translations in these volumes are not to be trusted."[9] Newman's review of Fox's edition of *Hildegard of Bingen's Book of Divine Works, with Letters and Songs* says: "the present book, like earlier Hildegard volumes from this press [Bear & Company], raises serious questions about the editor's integrity."[10] It is not a translation from Hildegard's original Latin version but from a German abridgment, which Fox erroneously calls "a critical text." Why did Fox not use the original texts?

Newman says the introductions in Fox's volume are "rife with errors about Hildegard's work," such as the false idea that she founded monasteries for men or administered a small kingdom. Instead of the feminist portrayed by Fox and company, Hildegard "firmly defended social hierarchies, and believed in divinely ordained gender roles," called God the Father and Son, and used masculine pronouns for God.[11] Neither was Hildegard a creation-centered theologian: "Hildegard's teaching is not creation centered at all; it centers on the Incarnation...."[12] Newman concludes her review by saying, "The wholesale misrepresentations that Bear & Company engage in cannot, in the long run, serve the cause of human integrity by purveying historical fallacies."[13]

Another critic is Simon Tugwell, O.P., who reviewed Maurice Walshe's edition of Meister Eckhart and Matthew Fox's *Breakthrough: Meister Eckhart's Creation Spirituality in New Translation* in the Dominican journal, *New Blackfriars*. Tugwell, proficient in Eckhart's thought and the Middle High

German language, devastates Fox's scholarship.

First, Tugwell reported the translation is of poor quality. Instead of using the Middle High German of Eckhart's original, Fox chose Quint's modern German translation of the original. Why did Fox not use the original language? Then Fox inaccurately translates Quint's text with "an extraordinary number of mistakes." At times he does not understand the syntax. At times he does not know the meanings of words. Tugwell says, "Sometimes it is difficult to avoid the feeling that the mistranslation is deliberate, intended to minimize anything that would interfere with the alleged 'creation-centeredness' of Eckhart's spirituality."[14]

The historical introduction "is so dominated by wishful thinking and sheer fantasy that the reviewer hardly knows how to begin criticizing it." When Fox alleged Celtic influence on Eckhart, Tugwell found himself reduced to "helpless, gibbering fury." He accuses Fox of "tendentious half-truths, or... downright falsehood."[15] For instance, Fox claims Eckhart was a feminist influenced by the beguine movement, but in fact no reliable evidence exists for either assertion. Also Fox calls Eckhart, a Dominican, "the most Franciscan spiritual theologian of the church" because he rejects the dualist thoughts of Platonist philosophers. In fact, St. Francis said that the soul lives in the body "like a hermit is a hermitage," or called the body and soul "both men" inside the person. Fox ignores this dualism in St. Francis, whom Fox has dubbed as "creation-centered." Tugwell has caught Fox in the trap of significant errors.

Unfortunately, the appeal and use of Fox's pseudo-translations are widespread. An American scholar visiting a shrine to Blessed Julian of Norwich in Norwich, England, stopped at the nearby gift shop. The racks displayed all of the Bear & Company translations. When the visitor explained how faulty and inaccurate these translations were, the clerk gushed, "That all may be true, but Fr. Fox has been such a help to my spiritual life."

Why are these criticisms significant for understanding Fox and Creation Centered Spirituality? First, they throw the rest of his scholarship into question. I certainly do not trust his biblical scholarship. Neither a Hildegard of Bingen scholar nor a Meister Eckhart scholar trusts his translations and commentaries. Experts find Fox committing mistakes in their specialties. Since Fox has betrayed his trust as a scholar, why should he be trusted?

Second, Fox builds much of his creation-centered theology on the foundation of Hildegard and Eckhart. His faulty translations support a crumbly theological edifice. Scholars can show that sacred Scripture, St. Hildegard, St. Francis, and even Meister Eckhart do not substantiate Fox's theology. To Fox goes the full responsibility for his dubious approach to "spirituality." An examination of Fox's theological propositions follows.

FOX'S WORLDVIEW

Two questions in the introduction to Fox's *Original Blessing* reveal an important insight into his worldview:

1. In our quest for wisdom and survival, does the human race require a new religious paradigm?
2. Does the creation-centered spiritual tradition offer such a paradigm?

As the reader may guess, my answer to both these questions is: *yes*.[16]

Like many New Agers, Fox borrows the idea of a "paradigm shift" from Dr. Thomas Kuhn, a historian of science. Kuhn describes how people make models of the universe to direct their interpretation of its events. Scientists often shape the basic models or paradigms by which people view reality, but they are as subject to paradigms as everyone else. Sometimes scientific discoveries so alter the old paradigms that they are abandoned for a new and more useful one. Such a paradigmatic shift occurred when science changed from the mechanistic idea of the universe associated with Sir Isaac Newton to Albert Einstein's world of relativity. Buckminster Fuller, Matthew Fox, and many others claim that the new Einsteinian paradigm has not yet been accepted. Once it is, a completely new way of viewing the world will dominate.

Fox is an evangelist of the inevitable new scientific, religious, and philosophical paradigm. Evidently, he wants to incorporate Catholic theology and spiritual traditions into the new paradigm. Not assuming that Catholic ideas have priority over the new paradigm, Fox says Catholicism must change to fit the new ideas. If the church does not adapt and lead the new way of thinking, "Mother Earth" will die, taking everyone down with her. How must the church change, according to Fox?

> To recover the wisdom that is lurking in religious traditions we have to let go of more recent religious traditions.... Specifically... an exclusively fall/redemption model of spirituality.... It is a dualistic model and a patriarchal one; it begins its theology with sin and original sin, and it generally ends with redemption. Fall/redemption spirituality does not teach believers about the New Creation or creativity, about justice-making and social transformation, or about Eros, play, pleasure and the God of delight.[17]

Fox identifies St. Augustine and the theology of humanity's fall into sin and the need for redemption as the prime culprit behind today's problems. Wars (especially nuclear wars), ecological crises, boredom, unemployment, and the rest of modern woes go back to St. Augustine's idea that people are born with original sin in their souls. Another culprit is Isaac Newton, whose mechanical paradigm compartmentalizes the world into disjointed, "piecemeal" entities. Fall/redemption theology leads to "sentimentalism and fundamentalism," focusing on personal salvation and a personal Savior.[18] As a result, people have "no ego, no self-respect, no tolerance for diversity, no love of creation, no sense of humor, no sense of sexual identity, or joy."[19]

Frequently, like the New Agers, his books decry society's and the church's emphasis on the brain's left hemisphere with its analytic, verbal, and logical processes. Fox wants people to incorporate the right hemisphere of the brain with its emotion, connection-making, mysticism, cosmic delight, maternity, silence, and darkness.

Fox's Paradigm. Fox believes his new paradigm will awaken the world to the cosmic dimension of reality. In it, Christ becomes cosmic, able to liberate everyone from the "bondage and pessimistic news of a Newtonian, mechanistic universe so ripe with competition... dualisms, anthropocentrism, and... boredom."[20] His translation of Eckhart says that all persons are "meant to be mothers of God." Everyone is called to give birth to the Cosmic Christ within themselves and society.[21] Then with Hildegard, Eckhart, and Carl Jung, everyone will know themselves to be "divine and human, animal and demon. We are Cosmic Christs."[22]

For Fox, the paschal mystery takes on new power in the Cosmic Christ context if people see it as the "passion, resurrection, and ascension of Mother Earth conceived as Jesus Christ crucified, resurrected, and ascended."[23] The Eucharist is "intimate," "local," and "erotic" when it becomes "the eating and drinking of the wounded earth."[24]

Among paradigm shifts in Christian belief and practice is Fox's idealization of feminist theology and rejection of patriarchal religion. He advocates a return to maternal religion, like that of many ancient native peoples throughout the world. Their "matrifocal religion" helps them reverence

God as a mother, the earth as our mother, the universe as our grandmother. They care for earth, seek justice, compassion, creativity, and harmony among people. He preaches this religious ideal as the new paradigm for everyone.

Is Fox a New Ager? It is hard to say. He borrows New Age ideas, like the paradigm shift, the threat of ecological disaster, and the need for a new religious and social paradigm. Like New Agers, he sets Newton against Einstein, the right brain against the left, and mysticism as the basis of religion, not dogma. He quotes New Age thinkers, like Fritjof Capra, Buckminster Fuller, and Starhawk the Wiccan. He suggests that the "contemporary mystical movement known as 'New Age' can dialogue and create with creation spiritual tradition."[25]

On the other hand, Fox criticizes New Age "pseudo-mysticisms," like interpreting "'past life experiences' in an excessively literal way without considering the possible metaphorical meanings." People dealing with "past lives" is an acceptable way to work out—"often in a very commendable and creative way—the deep suffering and pain from their present life."[26] While his interpretation of past life reading is not New Age, his endorsement of the practice, probably from a Jungian point of view, is unacceptable in Scripture and Catholic teaching. He writes: "All space and no time; all consciousness and no conscience; all mysticism and no prophecy; all past life experiences, angelic encounters, untold bliss, and no critique of injustice or acknowledgment of the suffering and death that the toll of time takes. In short, no body. To these movements the Cosmic Christ says, 'Enter time. Behold my wounds. Love your neighbor. Set the captives free.'"[27]

Again, he does not reject the New Age practices. He simply wants them balanced by social justice, conscience, and concern for the physical world. His response is to prophesy in the name of the Cosmic Christ that New Agers should love their neighbors and be just. The New Agers would probably agree and merrily go to a conference on saving the environment, crystals, or channeling.

Fox's analysis is inadequate. He does not go far enough in rejecting the occult practices of the New Age Movement. Commending witchcraft and shamanism in his institute encourages disciples to investigate the occult in the guise of learning "matrifocal" primitive religions to awaken the compassionate and creative mother in everyone.

Does he influence Catholics? It would seem so, especially women religious. The 1991 Franciscan Federation meeting of women religious superiors began with a woman dressed in Native American garb, carrying a bowl of incense and a feather. She walked to the north and invoked the spirit of the north with the incense. She repeated this ritual for the spirits of the east, south, and west. As a religious superior (who was appalled by it all) described these ceremonies to me, I recognized this rite as the opening of Wiccan ceremonies. What perplexes me is that Catholic nuns used it to open a meeting of superiors!

The 1991 National Assembly of the Leadership Conference of Women Religious also opened with the beating of drums. The religious superiors were led to the lower level of the building, which they designated as their "kiva," the name of secret society lodges of Southwest Native Americans. They chanted, "Come into the darkness," as they descended. Later they ascended from their kiva cave on escalators. These are just some of the new spiritual expressions which Fr. Matthew Fox and Starhawk the Witch, among others, have inspired. They bode ill for the religious communities who use them.

Certainly, Scripture summons us to be compassionate and loving and thirsty for justice. At the same time, it condemns the occult practices of native Canaanite religion, its mother goddesses Anath and Ashtarte, and its demand for human sacrifices (Dt 18:9-14). Furthermore, Starhawk's Wiccan (witchcraft) religion of the goddess is explicitly pantheistic and monistic.[28] Do Fox's frequent commendations of Star-hawk's work in re-awakening the goddess religion mean that he accepts pantheism after all? Clarifying his relationship to Starhawk's Wiccan thealogy (*thea* is Greek for goddess) would be helpful for the Catholic reader.

Fox's View on Astrology. Fox uses the standard New Age belief in the astrological ages, as ascribed to by Jung and others. Fox calls astrology a "tradition that offers us a glimpse into our own futures." But in the same section, he emphatically states, "What I present here is not my personal belief in astrology (I do not *believe* in astrology) but a method of seeing the human consciousness historically, where historical means both past and future."[29]

For Fox, astrology is a "symbolic method of seeing our futures" that "might have a valuable insight." Jung defends this view "by arguing that astrological wisdom is significant for what it tells us of the contents of our spiritual unconscious and, as such, needs to be taken very seriously."[30] Then Fox gives his version of Jung's description of two-thousand-year-long stages in human history: the bull (Taurus) from 4,000 to 2,000 B.C., representing "primitive, instinctual civilizations"; the ram (Aries), from 2,000 B.C. to A.D. 1, characterized by Judaism, conscience, and awareness of evil; and the fish (Pisces), from A.D. 1 to 1997, "dominated religiously by the figure of Christ." (Note that Jung claims the Age of Aquarius will begin 150 to 200 years from now; 1997 must be Fox's date.) The symbol of the two fish swimming in opposite directions "implies a dualistic spirituality that has so characterized Christian thinking and, in particular, Christian mysticism. It implies a Christ versus anti-Christ tension."[31]

Fox claims that the Piscean Age will close at the end of the twentieth century, "according to this theory, and if there is some truth to it" the Age of Aquarius is opening soon. It will be characterized by the symbol of water and "the deep," but he does not explain the significance of this further. In the New Age, "evil will be made conscious to every individual who may in turn be made truly spiritual and responsible." Individuals will have experiences of "the living spirit" in this spiritual age "where both the spirits of ugliness (evil) and of beauty (God) will be available to every person to choose in his own way."[32] He says it will also be an age of "reincarnation," not in the sense of transmigration of souls, which he rejects, but in restoring the sensual and incarnate sense again.[33] Fox foresees a changed church in the Age of Aquarius, too: "Sensual sacraments and liturgies, church leaders and schools, life-styles and working conditions—there lies the reincarnational church for a post-Piscean Age."[34]

As stated in the introduction of this book, the New Age gets its name from millennialistic tendencies that expect a transformation of society at the turn of the millennium. This belief motivates many people to join the movement because the changes are proclaimed as inevitable and irreversible. Since no one can stop the inexorable advance into the Age of Aquarius, everyone might as well join it willingly. Fox is convinced that the old Age of Pisces, with its dualistic, Augustinian, and Newtonian worldview is dead: "For the Constantinian era is dead and Neoplatonism is dead and Cartesian efforts to buttress up faith are dead and the Christian faith insofar as it has been known through these cultural patterns in the now dead-age [sic] of Pisces.... Some are scurrying to the East, others to the pagan West, still others to a wandering agnosticism or hollow reutterance [sic] of Christian formulas."[35]

I suspect that, like New Agers, he motivates himself and others to change their ideology and theology because he is convinced that a new Aquarian age is upon the world and the church. However, what if he is wrong? What if 1997 does not usher in the Age of Aquarius? The Catholic church has weathered many dramatic upheavals of society, from the destruction of Israel in A.D. 70, through the collapse of the Roman Empire, the Reformation, French Revolution, and the atheistic persecutions of the Marxists and Nazis. The church, the beloved bride of Jesus Christ, will survive until he returns for her, right on through the Age of Aquarius and beyond.

Fox does the world and the church a disservice by not teaching the whole of Scripture and accepting only parts. The Greek word for heresy means taking parts out of the whole. While Fox's love of creation and its God-given goodness is commendable, his new paradigm is not. It becomes a vehicle for Catholics to enter into the New Age Movement with a pseudo-Catholic sanction.

The influence of this hope for the end of the Piscean Age of Christianity and selective approach to Scripture showed up in another drumming ceremony at the 1991 National Assembly of the Leadership Conference of Women Religious. While Michael Mansfield beat a drum, Michelle Belto read out loud certain passages from Scripture that have been criticized by many in the feminist movement. After each passage was proclaimed, Mansfield chanted, "No, this is not the Word of our God!" Then the approximately nine hundred religious superiors and their assistants echoed back, "No, this is not the Word of our God!" The superior who reported this to me walked out after this desecration of two passages.

FOX'S TEACHING ON GOD AND CHRIST

As stated in the introduction, a central element in defining the New Age Movement is belief in pantheism, the idea that everything is God. Where does Fox's doctrine about God and Christ place him? Squarely in the kind of confusion that should not mark Christian teaching (see 1 Cor 14:33, "For he is not a God of disorder but of peace").

Explicitly Fox rejects pantheism, the belief that "everything is God and God is everything," as a heresy that removes God's transcendence and makes the sacraments impossible.[36] Instead, he holds to panentheism, which teaches that "everything is in God and God is in everything." This idea has its home in the late Neo-platonism of the Middle Ages, especially in the teaching of John Erigena, Nicholas of Cusa, and Meister Eckhart. Fox does not like Platonism, so he dubs these Neo-platonists "creation-centered theologians."

All three philosophers came under church scrutiny and even condemnation because their explicit claims of panentheism began to sound like pantheism. Matthew Fox has the same problem. His quotation of Nicholas of Cusa, according to the Bear & Company version, sounds like pantheism, though he calls it panentheism: "The absolute, Divine Mind, is all that is in everything that is.... Divinity is the enfolding and unfolding of everything that is. Divinity is in all things in such a way that all things are in divinity.... We are, as it were, a human deity. Humans are also the universe, but not absolutely since we are human. Humanity is therefore a microcosm, or in truth, a human universe. Thus humanity itself encloses both God and the universe in its human power."[37]

Also consider these quotes from Fox's version of Meister Eckhart: "The seed of God is in us.... Now the seed of a pear tree grows into a pear tree, a hazel seed into a hazel tree, the seed of God into God."[38] "I discover that God and I are one. There I am what I was, and I grow neither smaller nor bigger, for there I am an immovable cause that moves all things."[39]

These and similar passages throughout Fox's books bring an understanding of Christ and divinity rooted in Fox's translations and imagination rather than Scripture or church teaching. Sounding remarkably like Mark and Elizabeth Clare Prophet, Fox wants people to "birth" their own "I AM," which is the experience of the divine "I AM." The reason for our existence is to "birth the Cosmic Christ in our being and doing."[40] Fox believes that everyone can and should give birth to the Cosmic Christ, awakening the maternal within us. Sr. Uhlein promised this same thing in her talk at Loyola, saying that each millennium has its way of giving birth to Christ. Mary gave birth to Jesus Christ in A.D. 1; hundreds of European churches were built to honor Mary around A.D. 1000; now we will all give birth to the Cosmic Christ in A.D. 2000! Neat but unreal.

Fox's statements about the Cosmic Christ sound pantheistic, and it is hard to tell if he believes that Jesus is the only begotten Son of God. He writes, "The divine name from Exodus 3:14, 'I AM who I AM,' is appropriated by Jesus who shows us how to embrace our own divinity. The Cosmic Christ is the 'I AM' in every creature."[41] Again, Fox sounds like the Church Universal and Triumphant as he seems to say that Jesus appropriated his divinity and we can do the same. That makes Jesus no more divine than we are, as many New Agers teach.

Fox says we need to "let go of the quest for the historical Jesus and embark on a quest for the Cosmic Christ."[42] Yet the Cosmic Christ theology must not be believed or lived "*at the expense of the historical Jesus.*" Fox wants a dialectic or interchange of ideas between the historical and cosmic, so as to incorporate the mystical and the prophetic.[43] This requires a conversion from a "personal Savior" Christianity, which is "anthropocentric and antimystical" to a "Cosmic Christ."[44]

Which of Fox's statements do we believe? What is the basis for accepting his doctrine? He is confusing and contradictory. Perhaps he overemphasizes the need for the right side of the brain with its intuition, mysticism, and freedom from dualistic, either/or thinking, and the limitations of logic because of his own illogic. For many New Agers the emphasis on right hemisphere non-thinking is the perfect defense against logic, communication of ideas, the expertise of other people, and common sense. Fox's thinking mixes New Age ideas and clichés with sloppy translations of Scripture and medieval treatises. It may appeal to the right side of the brain, but it will not bear good fruit.

Are all of his concerns wrongheaded? Certainly not. Christians do need a better love of creation and the environment. Growth in compassion and creativity (in the analogous sense by which we creatures can be creative) is a wonderful gift from God. Passion for justice and concern for the poor are biblical characteristics. Yet none of these requires us to abandon the faith handed on to us by the apostles. We need not accept Fox's view that "the church as we have known it is dying,"[45] or that "Christianity as we know it will *not* survive for we know it now in wineskins that are brittle, old, and leaking."[46] Christ Jesus will renew the church in line with its past truths and bring many people to salvation through union with him in the Mystical Body, the church, the bride whom he devotedly loves.

NINE

What Is a Catholic to Do?

B ECAUSE OF THE GROWTH OF THE NEW AGE MOVEMENT outside the church and within it, Catholics have some basic
choices to make. We can bemoan the problem helplessly
and await the Second Coming of Jesus as the only possible
solution. Or we can respond to the New Age Movement with
fire, vigor, and creativity.

I hear many faithful Catholics whine in despair and wring
their hands because a New Age workshop was offered in
their parish or retreat center. No doubt these worried people have the faith, but they do not always display the virtue
of hope—hope that the Holy Spirit still moves within the
church or that the truth of the Catholic faith will prevail.
Sometimes faithful Catholics in responding to the New Age
neglect to show the virtue of love. Their anger and sense of
betrayal over the presence of New Age foolishness in
Catholic institutions dominates their responses. They do not
appear to love those involved in the New Age.

The introduction of false religious teachings and rites
into Catholic churches should stimulate legitimate anger,
but St. Paul calls us not to let anger take root in our hearts
when he writes, "Be angry, but sin not. Do not let the sun go
down on your anger, nor give a place to the devil" (Eph 4:26-
27). Instead we can say with Joshua, "As for me and my

household, we will serve the Lord." With so much to **do,** the sooner we focus on the task at hand the more we will **be** able to accomplish with the help of Christ and his church.

STRENGTHENING OUR LIFE IN CHRIST

First, we must live our Catholic faith fully open to the riches of God's grace. This means accepting a call from God through Jesus Christ in the power of the Holy Spirit. The Father is offering a gift of love to enable us to love God "with our whole hearts, minds, and souls." He calls us away from sin to a new life in Christ. We "put off the former conduct of the old human, corrupted because of the desires of deceit, to become renewed in the spirit of our minds and put on the new human, created according to God in righteousness and the holiness of truth" (Eph 4:22-24).

Concretely, our growth in Christ requires an active sacramental life and a daily prayer life to nourish our relationship with God. This is how God feeds, forgives, heals, and strengthens us in our vocations. God commands us to keep holy the Sabbath, which means weekly attendance at Mass. Of course, good preaching and liturgical practice are tremendous means of grace, but Jesus Christ is present at each Eucharist, even if the priest and ministers exhibit little personal devotion. Therefore, we come to receive Jesus Christ at Mass, listening to him speak to us through the Scriptures, especially the Gospels, and receiving him in the Blessed Sacrament. We can count on this double nourishment: being fed "by every word that comes from the mouth of the Lord" (Dt 8:3; Mt 4:4; Lk 4:4); and being fed by the flesh of the Word of God, Jesus Christ, which gives eternal life to all who receive it (Jn 6:27-58).

Archbishop Fulton Sheen frequently suggested prayer and meditation before the Blessed Sacrament as especially helpful. In this we come close to the person of Christ Jesus, who is present in a special way in the Blessed Sacrament. An hour a day seems like a lot at first, but after a while it seems only too short. Remember when in Gethsemane, immediately after the first Eucharist, Jesus asked his disciples, "Could you not even stay awake with me me for one hour?" (Mt 26:40; Mk 14:37).

In this hour with Christ, take time with the Scriptures, letting Christ speak to you through them. Read the whole of the Bible, especially the New Testament. Let the Gospels manifest Christ, who loves and challenges us. Aids in this regard are Frank Sheed's *To Know Christ Jesus* and Archbishop Sheen's *Life of Christ.*

As we hear God challenge our ideas and behavior, we may find ourselves to be sinners in his sight. Jesus' Sermon on the Mount and St. Paul's epistles contain moral instructions that challenge our behavior in order to draw us into deeper love of God and neighbor. Instead of turning to Jungian archetypes, astrology, or enneagram personality descriptions, the New Testament shows us ways to see ourselves before God. We can find ourselves in particular through prayerful, meditative reading of Romans 12-15, 1 Corinthians 13, Galatians 5-6, Ephesians 4-6, Philippians 3-4, Colossians 3-4, 1 Thessalonians 4-5, 2 Thessalonians 3, and Titus 2-3.

The ideals which God sets before humanity seem impossible to attain in this lifetime. When some people recognize that their actions, choices, and ideas are sinful, they despair of the possibility of perfection in this life and hope for many future reincarnations. Some New Age teachers convert disciples by denying the existence of good and evil, right and wrong, sin and virtue. They portray everything in life as educational, whether adulterous affairs, abortion, racial prejudice, neglect of the poor, or anything else affecting the *karma* of one's present lifetime. They deny that God judges anyone. Each person is his or her own judge, determining the next reincarnation.

When we Christians see ourselves falling short of the virtuous life God desires for his children on earth, he invites us to confess our sins in the manner Jesus instructed on the night of his resurrection (Jn 20:21-23). That is, he commissioned his apostles and their successors throughout the ages to forgive or bind sins. Jesus Christ offers the tremendous grace of recognizing our sinfulness and confessing our shortcomings and sins to his priests so that we can receive the power of forgiveness won on the cross.

Another antidote to New Age denials of moral principles and God's commandments is frequent reflection on biblical morality. Not only can we search God's Word to examine our own conscience, but we can learn to teach New Agers what the Lord says about being morally righteous, truthful, chaste, sober, and just to our neighbor. Christian morality is not grounded on personal opinions but the revelation of God's will.

When a New Ager teaches moral principles which contradict biblical and Christian morality, we can refer him or her back to God's Word. As I have mentioned earlier, whenever possible, it is best to ask the New Ager, the cultist, or the non-Christian to read the biblical passage to you rather than quote it or read it to him or her. Two things happen when they read the text to you: first, they are so occupied with reading that they cannot think about countering your arguments or ideas; second, the power of God's Word can affect them at a more personal level.

A healthy devotion to the Blessed Virgin Mary, firmly rooted in Scripture and the Rosary, can be a helpful element in our prayer life. By praying the Rosary we recall the key mysteries of our faith, meditating on the incarnation of God in Jesus, his death and resurrection, the sending of the Holy Spirit, and our hope to be with God forever in heaven. Mary's intercession and motherly care is a tremendous grace for ourselves and those to whom we witness, including the New Agers.

An active ministerial life is essential if we are to dynamically confront the New Age Movement. As novices we Jesuits learned ministry by cleaning the house. Scrubbing toilets, pots, and pans, and simple work around the community is the appropriate way to begin. Instead of scorning the small tasks, learn responsibility by doing them well. Then one graduates to larger tasks. God will open doors for more ministry and expand our horizons of service.

Ministry to the poor and needy is an especially helpful antidote to some of those New Agers who proclaim our right to have as much wealth as we can get. Contact with the poor sensitizes us to the needs of others, taking us beyond our own needs and desires, and putting them in a larger perspective. Furthermore, the poor have tremendous needs, which in itself is an impelling motive to serve them. Everyone who works with the poor comments on how much they have to teach us. Ministry to the poor, helpless, and sick should be part of our ministry.

ADDRESSING FALSE DOCTRINE

Along with these basics of the Christian life, an intellectual component is necessary to address the New Age Movement and cults. The hard work of reading Scripture and solid books of Catholic theology help us understand the gospel. Like bank tellers who learn to detect counterfeit money by becoming experts at handling real money, we will detect false doctrine most easily when we become more familiar with the real thing. Therefore, read good Catholic theology. Not all of it is impossibly difficult or limited to specialists. A number of lay people have written superbly clear books that explain the faith and the reasons to believe it.

C.S. Lewis was an Anglican who avoided the divisive controversies of Christianity and gave excellent explanations of the Christian faith. He is so successful as an apologist partly because he was an atheist who converted to Christ. While he presents the arguments for atheism, pantheism, and other philosophies fairly and well, he identifies their inherent flaws because he knew them from the inside. *Mere Christianity*, *Miracles*, and *The Problem of Pain* are especially good. But his novels and other books are also well worth reading.

Another commendable Christian author is G.K. Chesterton, a convert to the Catholic faith. His *Everlasting Man* and *Orthodoxy* are wonderful not only for their clear teaching of Catholicism but for their marvelous use of the English language. These can form the basis of theological studies, but do not stop with them. Keep finding solid books and read the ones that best suit your interests and abilities.

An important area of study is the science of apologetics. Many Catholics have written books defending the faith against its attackers. Mr. Frank Sheed is one of the best, especially in his classics *Theology for Beginners* and *Theology and Sanity*. Frs. Rumble and Carty have written a three-volume work, *Radio Replies*, which is popular. A well organized list of good theology and apologetic materials can be ordered from: Catholic Answers, 7290 Engineer Rd., Suite H, San Diego, California 92111 (1-800-345-0050).

Many apologetic books about the New Age Movement, mostly by Protestants, are excellent. They have borne the heat of the day in confronting and exposing the New Agers. I have included an annotated bibliography in this book to indicate which of these books I have found to be the best.

When one is already grounded in Christian theology, it is possible to read the New Age books themselves. Frequently audiences ask me, "Why bother with this step if their ideas are so wrong? Isn't this study dangerous? I feel like I am wasting my time by reading foolish nonsense instead of good Christian literature that nourishes my heart, mind, and soul."

At times it is dangerous, since it exposes the mind to subtly devised myths and philosophies. Yet unless one reads the New Age materials, one cannot confront them fairly. The Christian critic of the New Age Movement has to know what they teach before the precise logical fallacies become clear.

How much should one read of New Age materials? The norm I use is that I read to the extent to which I will be teaching and publicly criticizing certain New Age beliefs and practices. If I am not going to write or speak about them, I do not read New Age books or listen to tapes on such topics. For most Catholics, this norm probably means you only want to read what is necessary to defend the faith adequately. For example, if one of your Catholic friends is involved in the Church Universal and Triumphant (CUT), you may need to read one or two books by Elizabeth Clare Prophet, the guru of this cult, so you can refute its errors in discussions with your friend. Always remember to pray for God's protection when reading New Age books or listening to New Age tapes.

EVANGELIZING NEW AGERS

Hard study of the faith is indispensable, but it is not sufficient. Another step is the willingness to confront New Agers. Unless we take the risk of talking to them, they will probably not hear the gospel of Christ. We need not be belligerent and confrontational, slugging our way through New Agers at every psychic fair that comes to town. Remember that the Scriptures are the two-edged sword of the Spirit (Eph 6:17; Heb 4:12), not a bludgeon with which to club people over the head. Let God open the doors to witness to Christ Jesus and his bride, the church, and just walk in the doors he opens.

Here are some helpful tips for witnessing:

Listen to the New Agers. Draw them out by asking questions about their beliefs. Try to understand the logic behind their words. Ask how they got into the New Age. What is their story? Ask about their values. Usually people hold some positive values behind their New Age ideas, no matter how strangely it is manifested

Once I asked a satanic high priest why he worshiped the

evil one. He answered that he wanted to reconcile God and Satan because once they learned to get along, war, violence, and oppression would end. When I have told this story, some audiences have gasped and groaned in shock at his beliefs. That kind of reaction will turn a New Ager or cultist away. Instead, I commended his values. The abolition of war and violence is an excellent goal. His logic was a problem, though. After discussing that, he went to confession and renewed his baptismal vows.

Listen to know where a person itches, so you can scratch the right spot. Even when you are knowledgeable about a New Age practice or cult, try to hear why that particular person is involved in it. Then respond to his or her need with the authentic gospel of Christ.

New Agers set a high value on being open minded. That can be to your advantage if you invite them to be as open to Christianity as they want you to be open to their New Age position. Listen to them carefully, then ask them to open themselves to the gospel.

Look for the good in their ideas and relate it to the truth that God has already revealed. Build on the good that they have shared by relating it to Christ and his saving mission. Show them that their search is really for Christ.

Learn the scientific fallacies of New Age practices and point them out to New Agers or their converts. This sows doubt in their minds about the whole New Age system and opens them to you.

Many New Agers like to quote Scripture. It is part of our cultural heritage, and they want to integrate it into their worldview. However, they usually quote it out of context and sometimes add to the text. Show them the actual Scripture texts in their context and stop their pretexts for error.

Once again, it is better for them to read the passage to you instead of quoting the passage or reading it to them. Let the Holy Spirit, who inspired the Scriptures in the first place, stir their hearts with God's holy Word. His job is to convict and convert others. We are simply his instruments. Find the biblical texts that refute contradictory New Age doctrines in the apologetic books which address the New Age Movement. Remember that New Agers attack Christianity, blaming the church for the world's woes, for removing occult teachings from Scripture, and make many other accusations. They teach false views of God, Christ, the Holy Spirit, the church, and salvation. In responding to their attacks you present a "defense (*apologia*) to anyone who asks you a reason for your hope" (1 Pt 3:15).

When you do not know something, do not be afraid to admit ignorance. They will respect your honesty and trust you more. Also people get overly excited when they are ignorant. They tend to yell less when they are knowledgeable. An honest admission of ignorance may prevent a shouting match from taking place and keep the New Ager in a more receptive state of mind. Never forget how much they appreciate being mellow. Instead of getting angry, tell the person you will do your best to research the subject and get back to him or her with the results. See the appendix of groups to help in confronting cults and the New Age Movement in this and other books on the New Age. Locate the organizations and resources that will help you find the information you need.

WORKING TOGETHER

The preceding suggestions are directed to each of us individually. However, not all New Age activity takes place in one-on-one situations. What is one to do when a parish invites an astrologer or channeler to speak? What happens when a nun or priest or lay religious educator introduces New Age practices to a parish?

First, identify what is happening in the situation. Is it the occult? Wicca worship? pantheism? reincarnation? a false

Creation Centered Spirituality? enneagrams? Find out as much as possible about the problem at hand.

Second, go to the person responsible for the situation and explain your concerns and criticism. If you are not satisfied with the response, then speak to the pastor, director, bishop, provincial, or next person in rank and responsibility. Our Lord Jesus taught us that mutual correction demands that we address the offender personally before we escalate our tactics (Mt 18:15-17). But do give the person responsible a chance to respond and change *before* you escalate your tactics. The goal is not controlling the situation with our opinion but winning over our brother or sister to Christ.

Third, when necessary, take steps to counter the effects of the New Age, cultic, or occult event. For example, after an astrologer addressed a Catholic church group, a parishioner organized a lecture under parish auspices to criticize astrology. It took six months and a lot of work, but an even larger crowd attended the second talk. One woman said afterwards, "I was beginning to think I was crazy for not accepting the occult, but now I see that the church has not changed its doctrine on the occult at all." The pastor also attended the second lecture and learned, for the first time, that the New Age Movement was a serious threat to his people. He better understands the need to not let his church sponsor programs that undercut the Catholic faith.

A Matthew Fox protégé addressed a Texas catechism conference about Creation Centered Spirituality, teaching that while people are not God, they are emanations of God in a special way: "We are not God; we are gods." A few catechists were dismayed by the teaching but unsure about the exact nature of the error. They did not know what to do about it either. Given their limitations, they decided to meet weekly to study those lectures and other literature distributed to catechists. Every Sunday the group gathers before Mass to go over the materials and analyze them. By discovering that the literature contained misquotes or invented quotations to support a New Age leaning, these people have been able to call irresponsible leaders to task. I commend them for their diligent research, their desire to be fair and understand the other side of the issue, and their courage in speaking out. Especially commendable is their felt need for prayer together. Calling themselves the "Servants of Sheen" (after the late Archbishop Fulton Sheen), they turn to God for the grace to grow in charity toward opponents and for their conversion.

When some Louisiana Catholics learned that a Fox protégé was about to address their catechetics conference, they alerted pastors and participants. Not satisfied with being merely informational, they organized a day of prayer and fasting throughout the diocese for the day of the conference. The goal was a call to deepen their Catholic faith and strengthen orthodox teaching in the schools.

In California and Texas, Catholic lay persons have opened bookstores to make solid Catholic teaching available to people. One, a Mr. Vick Claveau, traveled from parish to parish in rural California to make books and tapes available. Mrs. Margaret Hotze and others started a Catholic bookstore in Houston, Texas. They sponsor lectures that counteract New Age influences. Mr. Terry Barber began St. Joseph Communications in West Covina, California (1-800-526-2151) to record Catholic apologetics lectures and market them at affordable prices. Another group of concerned lay persons started the St. Joseph Radio Show in Orange, California.

One gentleman heard one of my lectures on the enneagram and read my *New Covenant* magazine articles about it. When his parish was about to sponsor an enneagram workshop, he distributed the articles to parish council members so they could rethink the issue in light of more information. The seminars were not held.

Sometimes nothing can be done about New Age events taking place in parishes and retreat houses. Sometimes a director of religious education, pastor, or other leader will not budge. As related earlier, one woman did not want to teach her catechism class that short aspirations from Scripture were *mantras* (a Hindu term for short prayers). She was told that *mantra* just means a "short prayer," so it is okay to use. Since she was not convinced of her pastor's reasoning, he told her she would either teach *mantras* or not teach at all. She would not and was fired. The religious superior who attended the 1991 Leadership Conference of Women Religious had to walk out when about nine hundred of her fellow superiors chanted to a drum that certain passages of Scripture were "not the Word of our God." She walked out of other meetings that began with the chant, "Come into the darkness."

Our Lord Jesus taught that sometimes the only viable alternative is leaving the situation. When he instructed the apostles and disciples about their first missionary endeavor, he said, "When entering a house, greet it, and if the house is worthy, let your peace come upon it. But if it is not worthy let your peace return to you. And whoever does not accept you or hear your words, go outside the house or that city and shake the dust off your feet" (Mt 10:12-14). Jesus instructs us to pray for the peace of everyone to whom we are sent.

If they do not accept us or our prayer for peace, we can do nothing about it. Our responsibility is to pray for them and proclaim the gospel of Jesus Christ. If they cannot accept our peace, God will return it to us and we can go on our way. What we *can* do is perform our duty for the greater glory of God and leave the rest to him.

Yet leaving is not the only thing that one can do. First, it is always possible to write letters to the persons in charge to inform them about why you left or were asked to leave. A sober, gentle, and firm explanation about how the activity violated your conscience might be in order. In some situations it may be appropriate to send a copy of the letter to the local bishop. You may not get an immediate response. Do not worry about that. Do what you are able to do and put the rest into God's hands. But creating a paper trail can help those in authority make difficult decisions at a later time if the problems are repeated. If so, you will have been one part of the solution.

In these delicate situations, it is all the more important to work with other believing brothers and sisters. Their shared wisdom and insight is itself valuable. Praying and fasting for the circumstances seems less a burden if done with other Christians. Christ calls Christians to be his Mystical Body, his church. Therefore bear the problems of the church as a church, with fellow Christians. In this way our blessed Lord can draw from us the richness and diversity of gifts he has scattered among us for the sake of building up the whole body.

This is not a call to be obnoxious, nor is it a summons to mobilize against everything we do not like. Our liking or disliking some incidental is not the issue at stake here. Rather, will we stand up for what is truly the Catholic faith, or will we allow false doctrines to be taught? When the issue is merely a matter of personal taste, we should learn to accommodate and compromise, learning to work with a variety of people within the church. But when someone contradicts clear Catholic doctrine, then we have an obligation, whether we are clergy or lay, to stand up for the church and its faith. The Nazis gained power in Germany when good people did little or nothing to stop them. The New Agers will dominate American Catholics unless those who see the errors stand up to the falsehoods.

When we meet our Lord face to face, we want to be able to tell him that we used the talents we had to the best of our ability to serve him and his church, seeking only his greater glory in everything. Then he will tell us, "Come, enter into the glory of my Father's kingdom."

CONCLUSION

In closing, you should never feel you are handling the crisis of this growing movement on your own. You are not alone. As Catholics, we can have complete confidence that God our Lord and the whole heavenly court are with us. The gifts of the holy sacraments are available for closeness to God, forgiveness of sins, healing, unity in marriage, and strengthening for ministry. The Holy Spirit comes upon us in strength at our confirmation, enabling us to use gifts that are beyond our own abilities. St. Paul mentions some of these gifts of the Holy Spirit in 1 Corinthians 12 and Ephesians 4. Be open to the use of these gifts, especially words of wisdom and understanding (1 Cor 12:8). These gifts bring to mind things we forgot that we knew or inspire new thoughts in us to meet the challenge of the New Age worldview.

We need to pray for the New Agers, knowing that Jesus Christ wants them converted to himself infinitely more than you or I do. By nature he loves each person so much that he died on the cross for each one of them. You and I will never love the New Agers that much. Therefore, have confidence in Christ's love and the power of his grace to work in their hearts. God converts. We are merely his instruments. God is amazing in the ways he uses the things we say to convert people to him. Those surprises are great evidence that our Lord Jesus Christ ultimately is the Redeemer.

Groups to Help in Confronting Cults and the New Age Movement

American Family Foundation
Box 336
Weston, MA 02193
(617) 893-0930

Catholic Answers, Inc.
7290 Engineer Road, Suite H
San Diego, CA 92111
(619) 541-1131
For book orders: (800) 345-0050

Center for Christian Information
P.O. Box 5616
Santa Fe, NM 87502
No phone number could be found for this organization.
This is a Catholic group.

Christian Research Institute
Box 500
San Juan Capistrano, CA 92693-0500
(714) 855-9926

Cults Awareness Network
National Office
2421 W. Pratt Blvd., Suite 1173
Chicago, IL 60645
(312) 267-7777

Cult Hotline and Clinic
1651 Third Ave.
New York, NY 10028
(212) 860-8533

California address of group above:
6505 Wilshire Blvd.
Los Angeles, CA 90048
(213) 852-1234

Freedom Counseling Center
1633 Old Bayshore Highway, Suite 265
Burlingame, CA 94010
(415) 692-1403

Interfaith Coalition of Concern about Cults
711 Third Ave.
New York, NY 10017
(212) 983-4977

Spiritual Counterfeits Project
P.O. Box 4308
Berkeley, CA 94704
(415) 540-0300

Notes

Introduction

1. Marilyn Ferguson, *The Aquarian Conspiracy*, (Los Angeles: J.P. Tarcher, Inc., 1980), 62; see also her comments about drugs, 89-90, 95, 106, 110-111, 126.
2. Ferguson, *The Aquarian Conspiracy*, 31.
3. Ferguson, *The Aquarian Conspiracy*, 380.
4. Shirley MacLaine, *Dancing in the Light*, (Toronto: Bantam Books, 1985), 343.
5. Frances Adeney, "Educators Look East," *Spiritual Counterfeits Journal* 5, no. 1 (Winter 1981), 29.
6. MacLaine, *Dancing in the Light*, 41.
7. Ruth Montgomery, *The World Before*, (New York: Fawcett Crest, 1976), 14.
8. Montgomery, *The World Before*, 167.
9. C.S. Lewis, *Miracles: A Preliminary Study*, see chapter III, "The Cardinal Difficulty of Naturalism," (New York: Macmillan Publishing Company, 1947), 12-24.

ONE
Keeping up with the Gurus

1. Swami Anand Yarti, *The Sound of Running Water: A Photobiography of Bhagwan Shree Rajneesh and His Work, 1974-1978* (Poona, India: Poona Rajneesh Foundation, 1980), 382.
2. Swami Nikhilananda, *Vivekananda: The Yogas and Other Works*, Revised Edition, (New York: Ramabrishna-Vivekananda Center, 1953), 530.
3. MacLaine, *Dancing in the Light*, 339-340.
4. MacLaine, *Dancing in the Light*, 299-300.
5. MacLaine, *Dancing in the Light*, 350-351.
6. MacLaine, *Dancing in the Light*, 12.

TWO
In the Shadow of Dr. Jung

1. Carl G. Jung, *Memories, Dreams, Reflections*, recorded and edited by Aniela Jaffe, translated from the German by Richard and Clara Winston, Revised Edition, (New York: Random House, Inc., 1961), 94.

2. Jung, *Memories, Dreams, Reflections*, 42.

3. Jung, *Memories, Dreams, Reflections*, 70.

4. Jung, *Memories, Dreams, Reflections*, 40.

5. Jung, *Memories, Dreams, Reflections*, 39-40.

6. Jung, *Memories, Dreams, Reflections*, 98.

7. Robert T. Sears, S.J., "Jung and Christianity: An Interpersonal Perspective," *The Journal of Christian Healing*, Vol. 12, no. 2, 1990, 11.

8. Carl G. Jung, et al, *Man and His Symbols*, (London: Aldus Books in association with W.H. Allen, 1964), 309.

9. Jung, *Memories, Dreams, Reflections*, 162.

10. Jung, *Memories, Dreams, Reflections*, 200-201.

11. Jung, *Memories, Dreams, Reflections*, 209.

12. "Paracelsus," *The Oxford Dictionary of the Christian Church*, edited by F.L. Cross, (London: Oxford University Press, 1958), 1013.

13. Jung, *Memories, Dreams, Reflections*, 3.

14. Jung, *Memories, Dreams, Reflections*, 57.

15. Jung, *Memories, Dreams, Reflections*, 210.

16. Sears, *Jung and Christianity*, 12.

17. Sears, *Jung and Christianity*, 18.

18. Jung, *Memories, Dreams, Reflections*, 55.

19. Jung, *Memories, Dreams, Reflections*, 4.

20. Jung, *Memories, Dreams, Reflections*, 43.

21. Jung, *Memories, Dreams, Reflections*, 38.

22. Jung, *Memories, Dreams, Reflections*, 40.

23. Jung, *Memories, Dreams, Reflections*, 58-59.

24. Jung, *Memories, Dreams, Reflections*, 42.

25. Jung, *Memories, Dreams, Reflections*, 62-63.

26. Jung, *Memories, Dreams, Reflections*, 70.

27. Jung, *Memories, Dreams, Reflections*, 10.

28. Jung, *Memories, Dreams, Reflections*, 27.

29. Jung, *Memories, Dreams, Reflections*, 98.

30. Jung, *Memories, Dreams, Reflections*, 210.

31. Jung, *Memories, Dreams, Reflections*, 279.

32. Jung, *Memories, Dreams, Reflections*, 211-212.

33. C.G. Jung, "At the Basel Psychology Club," in *C.G. Jung Speaks*, ed. by William McGuire and R.F.C. Hull, Bollingen Series XCVII

(Princeton: Princeton University Press, 1977), 371-372.
34. Jung, *Memories, Dreams, Reflections*, 216.
35. Jung, *Memories, Dreams, Reflections*, 98.
36. Michael Fordham, "Four 'Contacts with Jung,'" in *C.G. Jung Speaks*, ed. by William McGuire and R.F.C. Hull, Bollingen Series XCVII (Princeton: Princeton University Press, 1977).
37. Jung, *Memories, Dreams, Reflections*, 98.
38. Jung, *Memories, Dreams, Reflections*, 45-46.
39. Jung, *Memories, Dreams, Reflections*, 57.
40. Jung, *Memories, Dreams, Reflections*, 94.
41. Jung, *Memories, Dreams, Reflections*, 171.
42. Jung, *Memories, Dreams, Reflections*, 93.
43. Jung, *Memories, Dreams, Reflections*, 56.

THREE
Astrology: Grounding the Stars in a Sense of Science

1. Dusty Sklar, *Gods and Beasts: The Nazis and the Occult*, (New York: Thomas Y. Crowell Company, 1977), gives a documented history of Hitler's involvement with the Germanen Ordnen and Thule societies, their roots in theosophy, as well the occult and astrological background for Hitler and the Nazis.
2. Michel Gauquelin, *Dreams and Illusions of Astrology*, (Buffalo: Prometheus Books, 1979), vi, 10-14.
3. Jung, *Memories, Dreams, Reflections*, 98.
4. Albert Oeri, "Some Youthful Memories," in *C.G. Jung Speaks*, ed. by William McGuire and R.F.C. Hull, Bollingen Series XCVII (Princeton: Princeton University Press, 1977), 3-10.
5. Oeri, "Some Youthful Memories" in *C.G. Jung Speaks*, 9.
6. Oeri, "Some Youthful Memories" in *C.G. Jung Speaks*, 9.
7. Vincent Brome, *Jung* (New York: Atheneum, 1978), 65, quoting H.F. Ellenberger, *The Discovery of the Unconscious*, 689.
8. Brome, *Jung*, 67-69.
9. Ray Hyman, "Scientists and Psychics," 119-141; James Randi, "Science and the Chimera," 209-222, in *Science and the Paranormal*, ed. by George O. Abell and Barry Singer, (New York: Charles Scribner's Sons, 1981). Both articles document the way that various charlatans have duped scientists, and scientists wanted to be duped sometimes.
10. Brome, *Jung*, 69.
11. Brome, *Jung*, 65.
12. Congregation of the Inquisition, July 30, 1856.
13. Gordon Young, "The Art of Living," an interview with Jung on

July 17, 1960 for the London *Sunday Times*, 443-452, in *C.G. Jung Speaks*, ed. by William McGuire and R.F.C. Hull, Bollingen Series XCVII (Princeton: Princeton University Press, 1977).

14. Georges Duplain, "On the Frontiers of Knowledge," interview for the *Gazette de Lausanne*, September 4-8, 1959, tr. by Jane Pratt, in *C.G. Jung Speaks*, ed. by William McGuire and R.F.C. Hull, Bollingen Series XCVII (Princeton: Princeton University Press, 1977), 412-413.

15. Carl G. Jung, "At the Basel Psychology Club" in *C.G. Jung Speaks*, ed. by William McGuire and R.F.C. Hull, Bollingen Series XCVII (Princeton: Princeton University Press, 1977), 372-373.

16. Jung, "At the Basel Psychiatry Club" in *C.G. Jung Speaks*, 375.

17. Duplain, "On the Frontiers of Knowledge" in *C.G. Jung Speaks*, 413-414.

18. Jung, *Memories, Dreams, Reflections*, 4.

19. Jung, *Memories, Dreams, Reflections*, 280.

20. Jung, *Memories, Dreams, Reflections*, 211.

21. Jung, *Memories, Dreams, Reflections*, 220.

22. Jung, *Memories, Dreams, Reflections*, 77.

23. Michel Gauquelin, *Dreams and Illusions of Astrology*, (Buffalo: Prometheus Books, 1979), 93; R.B. Culver, and P.A. Ianna, *The Gemini Syndrome: A Scientific Evaluation of Astrology*, (New York: Prometheus Books, 1984), 64-65.

24. George O. Abell, "Astrology" in *Science and the Paranormal: Probing the Existence of the Supernatural*, ed. George O. Abell and Barry Singer, (New York: Charles Scribner's Sons, 1981), 71-72.

25. Abell, "Astrology" in *Science and the Paranormal: Probing the Existence of the Supernatural*, 87-88.

26. Shirley MacLaine, *Dancing in the Light*, (New York: Bantam Books, 1985), 28.

27. Arnold L. Lieber, *The Lunar Effect*, (Garden City: Anchor Press/Doubleday, 1978).

28. George O. Abell, "Moon Madness" in *Science and the Paranormal: Probing the Existence of the Supernatural*, ed. George O. Abell and Barry Singer, (New York: Charles Scribner's Sons, 1981), 96-97.

29. Abell, "Moon Madness" in *Science and the Paranormal*, 98-99.

30. Abell, "Moon Madness" in *Science and the Paranormal*, 99-104.

31. Gauquelin, *Dreams and Illusions of Astrology*, 117-121; Abell, in *Science and the Paranormal*, "Astrology," 88-89.

32. Gauquelin, *Dreams and Illusions of Astrology*, 118-119; Abell, in *Science and the Paranormal*, "Astrology," 89.

33. Dr. Walter Martin, "Astrology," Audio tape C-05, (San Juan Capis-

trano: Christian Research Institute).

34. R.B.Y. Scott, *The Way of Wisdom in the Old Testament*, (New York: The Macmillan Company, 1971), 44, 111.

35. St. Augustine, *Confessions*, translated with an introduction by R.S. Pine-Coffin, (Baltimore: Penguin Books, 1961), 142.

36. St. Augustine, *Confessions*, 142.

FOUR
Tell Me Who I Am, O Enneagram!

1. Sam Keen, "A Conversation About Ego Destruction with Oscar Ichazo," *Psychology Today*, July 1973, 64-72; John C. Lilly and Joseph E. Hart, "The Arica Training," in *Transpersonal Psychologies*, ed. Charles T. Hart, (New York: Harper and Row, Publishers, 1975), 329-351; Claudio Naranjo, "The Enneagram: Stumbling Block or Stepping Stone?," Audio tape recorded at the Association of Christian Therapists, February, 1990, San Diego, California. Available through Diocesan Charismatic Renewal Center, 7654 Herschel Avenue, La Jolla, California 92037.

2. Naranjo, "The Enneagram: Stumbling Block or Stepping Stone?"

3. Lilly and Hart, "The Arica Training" in *Transpersonal Psychologies*, 342-344.

4. Naranjo, "The Enneagram: Stumbling Block or Stepping Stone?"

FIVE
Occult Roots of the Enneagram

1. Dorothy Ranaghan, *A Closer Look at the Enneagram*, (South Bend: Greenlawn Press, 1989).

2. Kathleen Riordan, "Gurdjieff" in *Transpersonal Psychologies*, ed. Charles T. Hart, (New York: Harper and Row, Publishers, 1975), 293; John G. Bennet, *Enneagram Studies*, (York Beach: Samuel Weiser, Inc., 1983), 2-3.

3. John G. Bennet, *Enneagram Studies*, (York Beach: Samuel Weiser, Inc., 1983), 89; see also 4, 32, 47.

4. Quoted in Bennet, *Enneagram Studies*, 75.

5. Sam Keen, "A Conversation about Ego Destruction with Oscar Ichazo," *Psychology Today*, July 1973, 64.

6. "Metatron" is the name of an archangel in the Hebrew Book of Enoch. He is called the "Prince of the Divine Presence" throughout the book. He claims to be the glorified Enoch whom God glorified and appointed ruler of the angels (4:1-5). See James H.

Charlesworth, ed. *The Old Testament Pseudepigrapha: Vol. I, Apocalyptic Literature and Testaments*, (Garden City: Doubleday and Company, Inc., 1983), 224-302, with particular information on Metatron, 241-244.

7. John C. Lilly and Joseph E. Hart, "The Arica Training" in *Transpersonal Psychologies*, ed. Charles T. Hart, (New York: Harper and Row, Publishers, 1975), 341.

8. Helen Palmer, *The Enneagram*. (San Francisco: Harper and Row, Publishers, 1988), 47.

9. Palmer, *The Enneagram*, 51.

10. Palmer, *The Enneagram*, 47, 51.

11. Claudio Naranjo, "The Enneagram: Stumbling Block or Stepping Stone?"

12. Keen, "A Conversation about Ego Destruction with Oscar Ichazo" in *Psychology Today*, 67.

13. Quoted in Riordan, "Gurdieff" in *Transpersonal Psychologies*, 284.

14. Keen, "A Conversation about Ego Destruction with Oscar Ichazo" in *Psychology Today*, 70.

15. Lilly and Hart, "The Arica Training" in *Transpersonal Psychologies*, 340.

16. Lilly and Hart, "The Arica Training" in *Transpersonal Psychologies*, 345-346.

17. Keen, "A Conversation about Ego Destruction with Oscar Ichazo" in *Psychology Today*, 64.

18. Lilly and Hart, "The Arica Training" in *Transpersonal Psychologies*, 342-343.

SIX
The Way out to Jesus

1. Marilyn Ferguson, *The Aquarian Conspiracy*, (Los Angeles: J.P. Tarcher, Inc., 1980), 31.

2. Ferguson, 62. See other examples of her view that drugs are an "entry-point" into New Age consciousness on 89-90, 95, 106, 110-111, 126.

3. The translation I used in this retreat followed the fourth-century Vaticanus manuscript and a few other texts. A number of Greek manuscripts (fourth-century Sinaiticus; later manuscripts and papyri) read, "Thanks be to God through Jesus Christ our Lord." Two fourth-century and some later manuscripts read, "I thank God through Jesus Christ our Lord." For this reason my reading, and the effect it had on me, may differ from other translations.

SEVEN
Catholic Involvement in the New Age

1. Katrina Raphaell, *Crystal Enlightenment*, Vol. 1 (New York: Aurora Press, 1985), 13-14.
2. Raphaell, *Crystal Enlightenment*, 13-15, preface.
3. Video tape, "Essence of Crystals."
4. Raphaell, *Crystal Enlightenment*, 45-47.
5. Judith Gaines, "Rock Power," *Chicago Tribune*, Section Five, May 22, 1988, 5.
6. Cheryl Lavin, "Thoroughly Modern Medium," *Chicago Tribune*, Tempo Section, October 31, 1990.
7. Jane Roberts, *The Seth Material*, (Englewood: Bantam Books, 1970), 271-272.
8. Roberts, *The Seth Material*, 207.
9. Ruth Montgomery, *The World Before*, (New York: Fawcett Crest Books, 1976), 40. *Edgar Cayce's Story of Jesus*, selected and edited by Jeffrey Furst, (New York: Berkley Books, 1968), 23-24.
10. Montgomery, *The World Before*, 46-47.
11. Montgomery, *The World Before*, 287-288.
12. Ruth Montgomery, with Joanne Garland, *Herald of the New Age*, (New York: Ballantine Books, 1986), 270.
13. J.Z. Knight, Videotape: "Ramtha and His Teachings" (Yelm: Ramtha Dialogues, 1986).
14. J.Z. Knight, Tape: "JZ on Ascension," (Yelm: Ramtha Dialogues, 1982).
15. J.Z. Knight, Tape: "JZ on Ascension."
16. Swami Anand Yarti, *The Sound of Running Water: A Photobiography of Bhagwan Shree Rajneesh and His Work, 1974-1978* (Poona, India: Poona Rajneesh Foundation, 1980), 382.
17. Swami Nikhilananda, *Vivekananda, The Yogas and Other Works*, Revised Edition, (New York: Ramabrishna-Vivekananda Center, 1953), 530.
18. Pat Rodegast, *Emmanuel's Book*, (Weston: Riends Press, 1986), 88.
19. Marilyn Ferguson, *The Aquarian Conspiracy*, (Los Angeles: J.P. Tarcher, Inc., 1980), 29.
20. Ferguson, *The Aquarian Conspiracy*, 381.
21. Shirley MacLaine, *Dancing in the Light*, (New York: Bantam Books, 1985), 203.
22. Leonard Orr and Sandra Ray, *Rebirthing in the New Age*, (Berkeley: Celestial Arts, 1977 and 1983), 247-258.
23. Walter Martin, *The Kingdom of the Cults*, Revised and Expanded

Edition, (Minneapolis: Bethany House Publishers, 1985), 248-249.

24. Walter Martin, general editor, *The New Cults*, (Ventura: Regal Books, 1980), 207-213.

25. Mark L. and Elizabeth Clare Prophet, *Climb the Highest Mountain: the Path of the Higher Self*, Book I, (Los Angeles: Summit University Press, 1980), Likenesses and Biographies of the Ascended Masters, inserted between 108 and 109.

26. Mark L. and Elizabeth Clare Prophet, *My Soul Doth Magnify the Lord: New Age Rosary and New Age Teachings of Mother Mary*, (Los Angeles: Summit University Press, 1979), 123-126; 135-145.

27. Prophet, *Climb the Highest Mountain*, 230.

28. Prophet, *Climb the Highest Mountain*, 228-229.

29. Mark L. and Elizabeth Clare Prophet, *The Science of the Spoken Word*, (Los Angeles: Summit University Press, 1983), ii.

30. Mark L. and Elizabeth Clare Prophet, *Saint Germain on Alchemy: For the Adept in the Aquarian Age*, (Los Angeles: Summit University Press, 1985), 313.

31. Prophet, *Saint Germain on Alchemy*, 316-320.

EIGHT
Matthew Fox and Creation Centered Spirituality

1. Matthew Fox, O.P., *The Coming of the Cosmic Christ*, (San Francisco: Harper and Row, Publishers, 1988), 169.

2. Fox, *The Coming of the Cosmic Christ*, 170.

3. Marvin H. Pope, *Song of Songs: A New Translation with Introduction and Commentary*, Anchor Bible (Garden City: Doubleday and Company, Inc., 1977), 385-386.

4. Matthew Fox, O.P., *Original Blessing*, (Santa Fe: Bear & Company, 1983), 46.

5. Matthew Fox, O.P., *Original Blessing*, 92, where Fox cites a lecture by Dr. Ron Miller at ICCS, Mundelein College, Chicago, January 18, 1982.

6. Matthew Fox, O.P., *On Becoming a Musical, Mystical Bear*, (New York: Harper and Row, Publishers, 1972), 66.

7. Fox, *Original Blessing*, 48.

8. Fox, *Original Blessing*, 62.

9. Barbara Newman, *Sister of Wisdom: St. Hildegard's Theology of the Feminine* (Berkeley: University of California Press, 1987), footnote, 250.

10. Barbara Newman, book review of "Matthew Fox, ed. *Hildegard of Bingen's Book of Divine Works, with Letters and Songs*," *Church History*, vol. 54 (1985), 190.

11. Newman, review in *Church History*, 191.

12. Newman, *Sister of Wisdom,* 250.
13. Newman, review in *Church History,* 192.
14. Simon Tugwell, O.P., book review of *Breakthrough: Meister Eckhart's Creation Spirituality in New Translation,* Introduction and Commentaries by Matthew Fox, *New Blackfriars,* vol. 63 (1982) 197.
15. Tugwell, review in *New Blackfriars,* 197.
16. Fox, *Original Blessing,* 9.
17. Fox, *Original Blessing,* 10-11.
18. Fox, *The Coming of the Cosmic Christ,* 151.
19. Fox, *The Coming of the Cosmic Christ,* 182.
20. Fox, *The Coming of the Cosmic Christ,* 135.
21. Fox, *The Coming of the Cosmic Christ,* 137.
22. Fox, *The Coming of the Cosmic Christ,* 138.
23. Fox, *The Coming of the Cosmic Christ,* 149.
24. Fox, *The Coming of the Cosmic Christ,* 214.
25. Fox, *Original Blessing,* 16.
26. Fox, *The Coming of the Cosmic Christ,* 45-46.
27. Fox, *The Coming of the Cosmic Christ,* 141.
28. Starhawk, *The Spiral Dance: A Rebirth of the Ancient Religion of the Goddess,* Tenth Anniversary Edition, Revised and Updated (San Francisco: Harper and Row, Publishers, 1979, 1989), 10-11, 22, 23, 27.
29. Matthew Fox, O.P., *WHEE! Wee, wee All the Way Home: A Guide to the New Sensual Spirituality* (Wilmington: A Consortium Book, 1976), ii.
30. Unfortunately, though Randy England's *Unicorn in the Sanctuary* (Manassas Trinity Communications, 1990), 122, quotes Fox's statement about astrological ages rather extensively, he omits Fox's denial of belief in astrology. England should have been more fair and directed the criticism more pointedly.
31. Fox, *WHEE! Wee, wee All the Way Home,* ii-iii.
32. Fox, *WHEE! Wee, wee All the Way Home,* iii.
33. Fox, *WHEE! Wee, wee All the Way Home,* 183.
34. Fox, *WHEE! Wee, wee All the Way Home,* 196.
35. Matthew Fox, O.P., *A Spirituality Named Compassion and the Healing of the Global Village, Humpty Dumpty and Us* (San Francisco: Harper and Row, Publishers, 1979), 256.
36. Fox, *Original Blessing,* 90.
37. Fox, *The Coming of the Cosmic Christ,* 126.
38. Fox, *The Coming of the Cosmic Christ,* 121.
39. Fox, *The Coming of the Cosmic Christ,* 154.
40. Fox, *The Coming of the Cosmic Christ,* 155.
41. Fox, *The Coming of the Cosmic Christ,* 154.

42. Fox, *The Coming of the Cosmic Christ*, 8.
43. Fox, *The Coming of the Cosmic Christ*, 79.
44. Fox, *The Coming of the Cosmic Christ*, 79.
45. Fox, *The Coming of the Cosmic Christ*, 31
46. Fox, *The Coming of the Cosmic Christ*, 149.

Glossary of Common Terms

Age of Aquarius
Astrologers believe that the earth is now, or will soon be precessing its axis out of Pisces into Aquarius and begin a new age. This new age will be characterized by greater consciousness, psychic powers, prosperity, and oneness among people and with God. (See precession.)

alchemy
The practice of medieval schools attempting to change base metals into gold. Jung believed that alchemy descended from gnosticism and he derived from it symbols of the transformation of the personality into psychological and spiritual wholeness.

anima
In Jungian psychology, it refers to the feminine figures who appear in men's dreams and symbolize their soul or subconscious.

animus
In Jungian psychology, it refers to the masculine figures who appear in women's dreams and symbolize their soul or subconscious.

archetype
Jung's term refers to forms without defined content that belong to the inherited structure of the human psyche. The archetypes manifest themselves in the motifs or typical images which recur in dreams, fantasies, myths, and fairy tales. (See Jungian Psychology.)

asana
Term for physical exercises practiced in *hatha yoga*.

Ascended Masters
In theosophy and its offshoots, these are the souls of the most enlightened individuals who ever lived. They contact certain humans (theosophists) to direct history. Many theosophists believe that the Ascended Masters will become incarnate again to initiate the Age of Aquarius.

astrology
Belief that the positions of the planets in relationship to the stars influence human behavior and destiny. The underlying principle of the planets' influence is, "As above, so below." (See zodiac.)

atman

(Sanskrit for breath) Hindu term for the individual soul, which was never born and never dies but appears in body after body through reincarnation. When it is capitalized, it refers to the universal soul from which all individual souls come. The *Upanishads* teach that *Atman* is *Brahman* and *Brahman* is *Atman*, thereby explaining their monistic understanding of the oneness of God and the individual soul. (See *Brahman.*)

bhakti

This type of yoga is characterized by love and devotion to particular gods. Union with the gods through love brings enlightenment and union with *Brahman*. The most popular form of *bhakti* yoga in America is the Krishna Consciousness Movement, devoted to the god, Krishna.

Brahman

In Hinduism, the impersonal ground of all being, being itself, from which every other object gets its being. Also, as *Brahman*, it is the name of the first of the three chief Hindu deities. (See *atman.*)

chakras

In *kundalini yoga*, the energy centers or psychic centers located on seven (or nine) points of the spine. By meditating, one can awaken the sleeping kundalini serpent at the base of the spine and draw it up to the top of the head, increasing one's level of enlightenment at each stage.

channeling

Contact between a human and a spirit, during which the spirit takes over or possesses the personality of the human. Often a different voice tone or accent will be heard. (See spiritism.)

chela

Hindu term for a disciple; it is frequently used by the Church Universal and Triumphant.

Church Universal and Triumphant (CUT)

A religion founded by Mark and Elizabeth Clare Prophet. They teach that the Ascended Masters of the Great White Brotherhood contact them to tell about the end of the world and about philosophical issues. (See theosophy.)

Cosmic Christ

The belief proposed by Fr. Matthew Fox, O.P., that Christ is a pre-Christian archetype of God being in every creature, the divine "I AM" in every creature and person, a divine pattern. Jesus incarnates the Cosmic Christ, "but by no means is [it] limited to that person."

Creation Centered Spirituality
Theological approach of Fr. Matthew Fox, O.P., which centers on the inherent goodness of creation and rejects the traditional Christian focus on the fall of humanity into sin and the need for redemption. He describes it as panentheistic, creative, compassionate, justice-seeking, ecological, feminist, and sensual, filled with ecstasy and eros.

crystals
A solid body composed of mineral compounds (like silicon dioxide in quartz) and shaped into symmetrical plane surfaces. Many New Agers believe crystal vibrates (millions of cycles per second) at the same rate as brain waves (two hundred cycles per second), thereby joining people with the universe. New Age claims are scientifically unfounded.

divination
Various techniques for learning the future of hidden knowledge. Most techniques are occult, like astrology, Tarot cards, *I Ching*, Ouija boards, and tea leaves.

ecliptic
The great circle of the celestial sphere that is the apparent path of the sun among the stars or of the earth as seen from the sun; the plane of the earth's orbit extended to meet the celestial sphere.

enlightenment
Spiritual or mental state of ecstasy or increased awareness.

enneagram
(Greek for a drawing of nine) Diagram composed of a circle with nine points on the rim, connected inside the circle by a triangle and a hexangle. Originally used for divination, it has become the symbol of a nine-personality-typing system. (See numerology.)

ephemeris
Table that identifies the location of the planets in relation to the constellations of the zodiac for each day of the year. Astrologers use it to cast horoscopes. (See horoscope.)

Fall/Redemption Theology
Belief that humanity fell from a state of grace because of Adam and Eve's sin and needs redemption from that fallen state. Jesus Christ, God incarnate, died and rose from the dead to redeem humanity. This is central to Christian theology but is rejected as the focal point of Christianity by Matthew Fox and Creation Centered Spirituality. (See Creation Centered Spirituality.)

gnosticism
Religious system from the beginning of the Christian era which

believed that salvation came from reaching or learning secret knowledge (*gnosis* in Greek). Such knowledge put one beyond the limits of the physical world.

guru
Hindu term for a spiritual leader, teacher, or master.

hatha
A school of yoga that uses physical exercises (*asana*) to attain enlightenment. This is the most common form of yoga in the West.

Hinduism
The dominant religion of India, though it has many sects. Because it developed over thirty-five centuries, no central dogma exists. It includes believers in pantheism, polytheism (up to three hundred and thirty million gods), agnosticism, and atheism. Most Hindus believe that the world is an illusion (*maya*) which is overcome by enlightenment. Reincarnation and *karma* are common ideas.

hologram
A three-dimensional picture made by the interaction of laser beams. Since any part of the picture reproduces the whole image, New Agers see it as a model for understanding monism. Each person is a part of the universe containing the whole universe.

horoscope
An astrologer's diagram showing the relative location of the planets and constellations of the zodiac on the day a person was born. This is used to describe personality or divine the future of the person. (See *ephemeris.*)

I Ching
Chinese "Book of Changes" which is used to divine one's fortune, either by throwing "yarrow" sticks or pennies. These sticks or pennies indicate a chinese ideogram of six lines, solid or broken or combined, each of which has a statement about one's fortune.

jnana
A type of yoga in which a person receives enlightenment through meditation on the knowledge of *Brahman* and in realizing that everything is *Brahman* (see the *Chandogya Upanishad* as an example of this early type of yoga).

Jungian Psychology
The school of depth psychology founded by C.G. Jung, a Swiss psychiatrist and former disciple of Freud. Jung accepted the importance of religion and spiritual matters for psychological wholeness. He used dream interpretation and the analysis of archetypes in his method. (See archetype.)

karma
Hindu term for the law of cause and effect. Whatever a person does in life will inexorably be repaid, either in this life or in another incarnation.

kath
In Sufism, the black spiritual center located at the belly. It (and *oth* and *path*) are similar to the Hindu notion of *chakras.*

kiva
The Native Americans of the Southwest, like the Pueblo, built kivas as ceremonial chambers for tribal associations.

kundalini
A school of yoga in which gurus help the disciples awaken the seven (or nine) *chakras* through various meditations and exercises. Hindus consider it a dangerous form of yoga that can bring illness or death unless used by well-trained gurus.

left brain
Because brain functions associated with rational thought, verbal expression, and logic were identified with the left side of the brain in the 1930s, New Agers call logical thought left brain. (See right brain.)

mandala
Sanskrit term for "magic circle." Usually it is a circle or square divided symmetrically into four (or its multiples) sections. Some forms of yoga meditate on it to focus the attention on a single point and empty the mind. Jung considered it an archetype that was very important in therapy as a symbol of wholeness. (See archetype.)

mantra
Short phrase or word from Hindu scriptures that is repeated many times. One goal is to empty the mind to dispel the illusion of *maya.* Others claim that repeating the *mantra* raises one's vibration levels and unites a person to the gods.

maya
Hindu belief that the external world is an illusion; only *Brahman,* the ground of all being, is real. One overcomes this illusion by yoga and attaining enlightenment.

monism
The metaphysical belief that all the differences among beings are not real but illusion; behind them all is a basic oneness of being.

nirvana
Buddist term for the state of enlightenment and bliss, in which one no longer has desire, passion, or the delusion of *maya.* Once at-

tained, a person is freed from the cycle of reincarnation because oneness with *Brahman* is reached.

numerology
A method of divining hidden knowledge by understanding the secret meaning of numbers and letters. This form of divination is used by central Asian practitioners of the enneagram. (See enneagram.)

occult
From a Latin word meaning "hidden, covered," this term refers to various forms of magic and divination.

Omega Point
Omega (the last letter in the Greek alphabet) stands for the end of time. According to Teilhard de Chardin, this Omega Point is the end of history drawing all things to itself, like a gravitational center. He believed that Jesus Christ was this Omega Point, drawing all things into himself. (See *Pleroma.*)

oth
In Sufism, the green emotional center located at the heart. It (and *kath* and *path*) are similar to the Hindu notion of *chakras.*

panentheism
Belief that everything is in God and that God is in everything.

pantheism
Belief that everything is God.

paradigm
It means a model or pattern, but New Agers use this to refer to one's model for understanding life and the world. Thomas Kuhn popularized this use of it in science. New Agers translated this new definition into the conclusion that a new model of thinking about the universe was inevitable.

path
In Sufism, the red intellectual center located in the head. It (and *oth* and *kath*) are similar to the Hindu notion of *chakras.*

Pleroma
(Greek for "fullness"). This term refers to the fullness of time as the end of the world. Teilhard de Chardin used it to mean the end time when Christ, the Omega Point, makes all creation one in himself. (See Omega Point.)

prana
(Sanskrit for "breath") This is the breath or life-force, according to Hinduism. It also refers to the breathing exercises meant to teach one how to absorb this life-force.

precession
A comparatively slow gyration of the rotational axis of a spinning body about another line intersecting it, so as to describe a cone caused by the application of a torque tending gradually to change the direction of the rotational axis. In astrology, it is applied to the rotational axis of the earth slowly changing direction and continuing to point to a particular constellation of the zodiac for a long period of time. Astrologers designate each age of the zodiac as the two thousand one-hundred and sixty years in which the earth points toward a particular constellation. (See Age of Aquarius.)

psycho-technology
A term used by Marilyn Ferguson and other New Agers for the techniques of altering one's state of consciousness.

Qu'tub
(Arabic for pillar). This is the name of key spirits contacted by George Gurdjieff and Oscar Ichazo, key figures in the spread of the enneagram. (See enneagram.)

raja yoga
The highest form of yoga, it is yoga or right thought, mind control, and physical exercises, in which the soul understands itself clearly and is united to *Brahman*, the ground of all being.

reincarnation
Belief that after death one's soul returns to earth in another body. (See *samsara*.)

right brain
Because psychologists in the 1930s identified certain intuitive functions on the right hemisphere of the brain, New Agers associate it with creativity, intuition, and enlightenment. (See left brain.)

samadhi
Hindu term for the state of enlightenment or bliss, in which one feels at one or in union with *Brahman*, that is, with everything that exists. This bliss is often the experiential basis for monism and pantheism. (See monism and pantheism.)

samsara
This is known as the wheel of reincarnation. Because people have bad *karma*, they have to return to earth repeatedly in new bodies. The goal is liberation from the physical world and absorption into *Brahman*. (See reincarnation.)

satanism
The worship of and commitment to Satan.

shaman
Native Siberian word for medicine man or witch doctor, which is also used to describe these roles among other peoples.

siddha
A type of yoga that teaches its students how to get psychic powers like levitation, flying in the air, and speaking in tongues. Transcendental Meditation is considered a *siddha yoga* that uses repeated *mantras* to get powers of flying (actually, hopping while in a seated position).

spiritism
The belief and practice of contacting the spirits of the dead. Today it is called channeling. However, unlike channeling, classical spiritism did not entail possession of the medium by the spirits but manifestations outside the medium's own body. Usually it was to help the living contact dead relatives or friends. (See channeling.)

Sufism
The general name for various schools of mysticism among Muslims. Many orthodox Muslims do not accept Sufi doctrines or practices, partly because they have been influenced by Hindu yogism. (See *kath*, *oth*, and *path*.)

tantra
A school of yoga that uses disciplines of sensual pleasure, especially sexual experience, to attain spiritual enlightenment. These practices are rooted in fertility cults and shamanistic magic, but the systematic and philosophic control distinguishes it from ordinary shamanism.

Tarot cards
A deck containing seventy-eight cards is used to divine information about someone's personality and future. The person picks out cards from the deck and the "reader" interprets their meaning.

theosophy
From Greek words meaning the Wisdom of God. Ancient theosophy schools believed in direct mystical knowledge of God and the world, pantheism, and the evolution of all beings. H.P. Blavatsky began a new tradition of theosophy in 1875, which she claimed to learn from the Ascended Masters of the Great White Brotherhood. Many groups have sprung from it, like the Church Universal and Triumphant. (See Church Universal and Triumphant.)

Upanishads
Following the *Vedas*, this collection of books forms the second layer of Hindu scriptures, written from the ninth century B.C. to the first century A.D. Yoga gurus composed these books to teach their methods of meditation, breathing, and exercise.

Vedas
The oldest Hindu scriptures, written by the Aryan conquerors of India around 1500 B.C. This material is mostly written from the perspective of the *Brahmin* priests and tells them how to offer sacrifices or comments on this. Many *mantras* or prayers come from the *Vedas*.

Wicca
Old English term for witchcraft. Many modern witches prefer it because it does not have as negative a connotation as witchcraft. It emphasizes an earth mother or goddess worship and should not be confused with satanism.

yoga
(Sanskrit for "yoke" or "union") In Hinduism, the general category of various kinds of disciplines meant to unite a person with the divine. Yoga can refer to physical (*hatha*), mental (*raja*), sexual (*tantra*), or other disciplines to achieve enlightenment.

zodiac
The band of twelve constellations (16 degrees wide), with the earth's ecliptic around the sun as its middle line. Observation of the relation of the planets to these twelve constellations is the basis of astrology. (See ecliptic.)

Bibliography

BIBLICAL MATERIAL

Scott, R.B.Y. *The Way of Wisdom in the Old Testament.* (New York: The Macmillan Company, 1971).

Charlesworth, James H. ed. *The Old Testament Pseudepigrapha: Vol. I, Apocalyptic Literature and Testaments.* (Garden City: Doubleday and Company, Inc., 1983).

CHRISTIAN BOOKS CRITICIZING THE NEW AGE MOVEMENT

There is not much Catholic literature on this topic, but Evangelicals and Fundamentalists have written a lot, of varying quality.

Not Recommended:

Cumbey, Constance. *The Hidden Dangers of the Rainbow.* (Shreveport: Huntington House, 1983). Cumbey pioneered criticism of the New Age by researching the pioneers of the movements and their books. Her information can be helpful to the careful reader. However, her critique depends too heavily on esoteric New Age writers, like Alice Bailey. She also makes many non-New Agers guilty by association with terms that could be New Age. She tends to see a New Age conspiracy in too many places.

England, Randy. *Unicorn in the Sanctuary.* (Manassas: Trinity Communications, 1990). England presents a lot of information about New Age infiltration into the Catholic church, with some ideas on ways for the laity to stem the tide. But he overstates some things and tends to hold a conspiracy approach.

Hunt, Dave. *Peace, Prosperity and the Coming Holocaust;* (Eugene: Harvest House, 1983); *The Seduction of Christianity.* (Eugene: Harvest House, 1985) Hunt tends toward sensationalism and has to be read carefully, though he often has interesting information on outlandish New Age material. However, he seems to reject much of its culture as not redeemable.

Recommended:

Baer, Randall N. *Inside the New Age Nightmare.* (Lafayette: Huntington House, Inc., 1989). This is a good testimonial by a leader of the New Age Movement who left it for evangelical Christianity. He is clear and simple in explaining its attraction and failure.

Groothuis, Douglas. *Unmasking the New Age.* (Downers Grove: Intervarsity Press, 1986). *Confronting the New Age.* (Intervarsity Press, 1988). He is a serious commentator who organizes his information clearly. His apologetic responses are usually solid, though he has an Evangelical soteriology, of course.

Hoyt, Karen. *New Age Rage.* (Old Tappan: Revell, 1987). This is a highly recommended introduction.

LeBar, Rev. James. *Cults, Sects, and the New Age.* (Huntington: Our Sunday Visitor Publishing, 1989). While the book focuses more on the cults than on the New Age Movement, it offers very valuable information to combat these influences. Also the church documents related to cults and sects are very helpful.

Martin, Dr. Walter. *The Kingdom of the Cults.* Revised and Expanded Edition. (Minneapolis: Bethany House Publishers, 1985).

_____. *The New Age Cult.* (Minneapolis: Bethany House Publishers, 1989).

_____. *The New Cults.* (Ventura: Regal Books, 1980). Walter's Evangelical soteriology always comes through, but he has good information on many of the cults and the New Age Movement. He supplies Scriptures to help in defending the Christian position.

Rath, Ralph. *The New Age: A Christian Critique.* (South Bend: Greenlawn Press, 1990). This is a good overview of the New Age Movement. Especially helpful to Catholic readers is Rath's attention to Catholic issues and sources to criticize New Age thought.

Reisser, Dr. Paul, Reisser, Terri, and Weldon, John. *New Age Medicine.* (Downers Grove: Intervarsity Press, 1983). The authors critique holistic medical treatments proposed by the New Age, both theologically and scientifically. At times they worry about the possible ramifications of New Age thought when the evidence is not clear.

Smith, F. LaGard. *Out on a Broken Limb.* (Eugene: Harvest House, 1986). A popular critique of Shirley MacLaine's books and media expressions of New Age.

Steichen, Donna. *Ungodly Rage: The Hidden Face of Catholic Feminism.* (San Francisco: Ignatius Press, 1991). This excellent book describes the presence of many New Age ideas among Catholic feminists, especially women religious.

SCIENCE AND NEW AGE

Abell, George O. and Singer, Barry. ed. *Science and the Paranormal: Probing the Existence of the Supernatural.* (New York: Charles Scribner's Sons, 1981). This collection of essays by scientists attacks the lack of reason and scientific method in the New Age Movement. It is very helpful for debunking the scientific claims of New Agers.

ASTROLOGY

Culver, R.B. and Ianna, P.A. *The Gemini Syndrome: A Scientific Evaluation of Astrology.* (New York: Prometheus Books, 1984).

Gauquelin, Michel. *Dreams and Illusions of Astrology.* (Buffalo: Prometheus Books, 1979).

Jerome, Lawrence E. *Astrology Disproved.* (Buffalo: Prometheus Books, 1977).

Lieber, Arnold L. *The Lunar Effect.* (Garden City: Anchor Press/ Doubleday, 1978).

Macneice, Louis. *Astrology.* (London: Aldus Books, 1964). An easy-to-read history and description of astrology, in general favorable to it.

Martin, Dr. Walter. "Astrology," Audio tape C-05, (San Juan Capistrano: Christian Research Institute).

Moore, Thomas. *The Planets Within: Marsilio Ficino's Astrological Psychology.* (London and Toronto: Associated University Press, 1982). An example of Jungian interpretation of psychology and astrology.

Zambelli, Paola. *'Astrologi hallucinati': Stars and the End of the World in Luther's Time.* (Berlin: Walter de Gruyter, 1986). A very scholarly history of astrology in medieval and Renaissance times. The articles describe the Catholic and Protestant theologians who believed in astrology as part of the accepted science of their times and how they accommodated it to Christian theology.

C.G. JUNG

Brome, Vincent. *Jung.* (New York: Atheneum, 1978).

Jung, C.G. et. al. *Man and His Symbols.* (London: Aldus Books in association with W.H. Allen, 1964).

Jung, C.G. Recorded and edited by Aniela Jaffe. *Memories, Dreams and Reflections.* Translated by Richard and Clara Winston. (New York: Vintage Books, a Division of Random House, 1965).

McGuire, William, and Hull, R.F.C. *C.G. Jung Speaking: Interviews and Encounters.* (Princeton: Princeton University Press, 1977).

Progoff, Ira. *Jung, Synchronicity, and Human Destiny.* (New York: Dell Publishing Co., Inc., 1973).

Stein, Murray and Moore, Robert L. eds. *Jung's Challenge to Contemporary Religion.* (Wilmette: Chiron Publication, 1987).

ENNEAGRAM

Anderson, Margaret. *The Unknown Gurdjieff.* (London: Routledge and Kegan Paul, 1962). A description of life among Gurdjieff's disciples and their devotion to his method.

Bennet, John G. *Enneagram Studies.* (York Beach: Samuel Weiser, Inc., 1983). Bennet was a disciple of Gurdjieff who lived with him for a while. He researched Sufism and writes about the historical roots of the enneagram.

Gurdjieff, George I. *Herald of Coming Good.* (New York: Samuel Weiser, Inc., 1973). His first book, stating some of his philosophy.

The following three books are known as *All and Everything,* in three series:

_____. *Beelzebub's Tales to His Grandson.* 3 vols. First Series. (London: Routledge and Kegan Paul, 1976). More of his philosophy, meant to introduce people to the strangeness of his ideas and "destroy, mercilessly... the beliefs and views... about everything existing in the world."

_____. *Meetings with Remarkable Men.* Second Series. (London: Routledge and Kegan Paul, 1977). This is an autobiography meant to use stories about his life to give a new vision "required for a new creation."

_____. *Life Is Real Only Then, When "I Am."* Third Series. (New York: E.P. Dutton, 1975). An introduction and a series of lectures to continue teaching what he means about the real world rather than the world of illusion we presently believe in.

Keen, Sam. "A Conversation about Ego Destruction with Oscar Ichazo," *Psychology Today,* July 1973, 64-72. This is an interview with Ichazo, one of the few places where he speaks about himself.

Lilly, John C. and Hart, Joseph E. "The Arica Training," in *Transpersonal Psychologies,* ed. Charles T. Hart. (New York: Harper and Row, Publishers, 1975), 329-351. This article gives further background to Ichazo, including information about occult practices in his group and the group's strong attachment to him.

Naranjo, Claudio. "The Enneagram: Stumbling Block or Stepping Stone?" Audio tape recorded at the Association of Christian Therapists, February, 1990, San Diego, California. Available through Diocesan Charismatic Renewal Center, 7654 Herschel Avenue, La Jolla, California 92037. This talk is a rare history of the enneagram's roots in Ichazo's and Naranjo's own teachings.

Ouspensky, P.D. *The Fourth Way: A Record of Talks and Answers to Questions Based on the Teachings of G.I. Gurdjieff.* (New York: Random House, 1957).

_____. *In Search of the Miraculous: Fragments of an Unknown Teaching.* (New York: Harcourt, Brace and World, 1949). Though the enneagram symbol is taught in Ouspensky's books, one searches in vain for information about the enneagram of personality.

Palmer, Helen. *The Enneagram.* (San Francisco: Harper and Row, Publishers, 1988). A popular version of the enneagram that spells out the various types.

Riordan, Kathleen. "Gurdjieff," in *Transpersonal Psychologies,* ed. Charles T. Hart. (New York: Harper and Row, Publishers, 1975), 281-328. A short background to Gurdjieff's thought.

Riso, Don Richard. *Personality Types: Using the Enneagram for Self-*

Discovery. (Boston: Houghton Mifflin Company, 1987).

_____. *Understanding the Enneagram: The Practical Guide to Personality Types.* (Boston: Houghton Mifflin Company, 1990). Riso tries to use more of a psychological approach but he has not given outside proof for the system or his own results, as he admits.

Speeth, Kathleen Riordan and Friedlander, Ira. *Gurdjieff: Seeker of the Truth.* Bibliography compiled by Walter Driscoll. (New York: Harper and Row, Publishers, 1980). This is the most orderly biography of Gurdjieff that I know of. The chronology is helpful and the bibliography is excellent for research purposes.

Wagner, Jerome. "A Descriptive, Reliability, and Validity Study of the Enneagram Personality Typology," Ph.D., 1979, Loyola University, Chicago.

_____. "Reliability and Validity Study of a Sufi Personality Typology: The Enneagram," *Journal of Clinical Psychology*, vol. 39 (1983), 712-717.

Waldberg, Michael. *Gurdjieff: An Approach to His Work.* Translated by Steve Cox. (London: Routledge and Kegan Paul, 1981). A good summary of Gurdjieff's ideas arranged topically.

CHANNELING

Cayce, Hugh Lynn. *The Incredible Story of Edgar Cayce.* (New York: Coronet Communications, Inc., 1964).

Dixon, Jeanne. *My Life and Prophecies.* As told to René Noorbergen. (New York: William Morrow and Company, Inc., 1969).

Furst, Jeffrey. ed. *Edgar Cayce's Story of Jesus.* (New York: Berkley Books, 1968).

Knight, J.Z. *A State of Mind: My Story.* (New York: Warner Books, 1987).

_____. Tape: "JZ on Ascension." (Yelm: Ramtha Dialogues, 1982).

_____. Videotape: "Ramtha and His Teachings." (Yelm: Ramtha Dialogues, 1986).

Langley, Noel and Cayce, Hugh Lynn. eds. *Edgar Cayce on Reincarnation.* (New York: Castle Books, 1967).

Lazaris. Tape: "Abundance and Prosperity: The Skill." (Fairfax: Concept Synergy, 1986).

_____. Tape: "Healing: The Nature of Health." Part I and II.

(Fairfax: Concept Synergy, 1986).

_____. Tape: "The Secrets of Manifesting What You Want." (Fairfax: Concept Synergy, 1986).

MacLaine, Shirley. *Dancing in the Light.* (New York: Bantam Books, Inc., 1985).

_____. *Out on a Limb.* (New York: Bantam Books, Inc., 1983).

Montgomery, Ruth. *Aliens among Us.* (New York: Ballantine Books, 1985).

_____. *Herald of the New Age.* With Joanne Garland. (New York: Ballantine Books, 1986). This is an authorized biography, telling how she became involved in spiritism.

_____. *The World Before.* (New York: Ballantine Books, 1976).

Roberts, Jane. *The Seth Material.* (Englewood: Bantam Books, 1970).

Stearn, Jess. *Edgar Cayce—The Sleeping Prophet.* (New York: Bantam Books, 1967).

CHURCH UNIVERSAL AND TRIUMPHANT

Prophet, Mark and Elizabeth Clare. *Climb the Highest Mountain: the Path of the Higher Self.* Book I. (Los Angeles: Summit University Press, 1980).

_____. *My Soul Doth Magnify the Lord: New Age Rosary and New Age Teachings of Mother Mary.* (Los Angeles: Summit University Press, 1983).

_____. *The Science of the Spoken Word.* (Los Angeles: Summit University Press, 1983).

_____. *Saint Germain on Alchemy: For the Adept in the Aquarian Age.* (Los Angeles: Summit University Press, 1985).

NEW AGE TECHNIQUES

Orr, Leonard and Ray, Sandra. *Rebirthing in the New Age.* (Berkeley: Celestial Arts, 1977 and 1983).

CREATION CENTERED SPIRITUALITY

Fox, Matthew. *The Coming of the Cosmic Christ.* (San Francisco: Harper and Row, Publishers, 1988).

_____. *On Becoming a Musical, Mystical Bear*. (New York: Harper and Row, Publishers, 1972).

_____. *Original Blessing*. (Santa Fe: Bear & Company, 1983).

_____. *A Spirituality Named Compassion and the Healing of the Global Village, Humpty Dumpty and Us*. (San Francisco: Harper and Row, Publishers, 1979).

_____. *WHEE! Wee, wee All the Way Home: A Guide to the New Sensual Spirituality*. (Wilmington: A Consortium Book, 1976).

Newman, Barbara. Book review of "Matthew Fox, ed. *Hildegard of Bingen's Book of Divine Works, with Letters and Songs*." *Church History*, vol. 54 (1985).

_____. *Sister of Wisdom: St. Hildegard's Theology of the Feminine*. (Berkeley: University of California Press, 1987).

Starhawk. *The Spiral Dance: A Rebirth of the Ancient Religion of the Goddess*. Tenth Anniversary Edition, Revised and Updated. (San Francisco: Harper and Row, Publishers, 1979, 1989).

Tugwell, O.P., Simon. Book review of *Breakthrough: Meister Eckhart's Creation Spirituality in New Translation*, Introduction and Commentaries by Matthew Fox. *New Blackfriars*, vol. 63 (1982), 197.